In Steadfast Love

LETTERS ON THE
SPIRITUAL LIFE

In Steadfast & LOVE

Letters On the *Spiritual Life*

Melannie Svoboda, SND

Sister Melannie Svoboda, SND

TWENTY
THIRD 23rd
PUBLICATIONS

Dedication

The following sisters served in leadership with me
during my years as provincial.
I dedicate this book to them
in gratitude for their steadfast love.

Mary John Paul Bobak, SND   Helen Louise Kist, SND

Josephe Fernandez, SND   Joanne Miller, SND

Jacquelyn Gusdane, SND   Virginia Reesing, SND

Margaret Harig, SND   Maureen Spillane, SND

Margaret Hess, SND   Valerie Sweeney, SND

Jean Hoelke, SND   Patricia Teckman, SND

Sally Huston, SND   Regina Zeleznik, SND

The author is grateful for the permission to quote from the following publications:

Rabindranath Tagore. *Gitanjali.* New Delhi: Macmillan India Ltd (1966, 1985).

Carol Lynn Pearson. "The Price." *The Search.* www.clpearson.com.

Marilyn Chandler McEntyre. "To Recognize Grace." *Weavings: A Journal of the Christian Spiritual Life.* July/August 2002, Vol XVII, No. 4. Upper Room Ministries. (Weavings: 1-800-925-6847)

Andrea Ayvazian. "The Only Sermon." *Sojourners Magazine,* November/ December 2003.

Twenty-Third Publications
A Division of Bayard
One Montauk Avenue, Suite 200
New London, CT 06320
(860) 437-3012 or (800) 321-0411
www.23rdpublications.com

ISBN 978-1-58595-628-9
Library of Congress Catalog Card Number: 2006939021
Printed in the U.S.A.

Contents

Introduction   1

1   Abounding in Steadfast Love   3

2   Notes and Poems from India   8

3   Higher, Higher! More, More!   13

4   Mary's Annunciation   18

5   Fear and Peace at Easter   21

6   Prayer of Thanksgiving for
All the Seasons of Our Lives   24

7   "One Wild and Precious Life"   26

8   The God Who Calls   30

9   Eleven Truths about Love   34

10   Seven Deadly "Isms"   37

11   What Is Freedom?   41

12   Jesus, the Master of Metaphor   44

13   The Common Good, Commitment,
and Charism   47

14   Thanksgiving and the Paschal Mystery   52

15   Saint Joseph   57

16   Pain and the Call to Transformation   60

17   Our Christian Legacy of Joy and Laughter   65

18   What Is God's Name?   70

19	Notes from South Korea	78
20	Border Crossings	84
21	Celibacy and Homelessness	89
22	I Have Never Seen the Face of God	94
23	The Sacredness of Creation	96
24	In Praise of Vulnerability	100
25	Against the Horizon of the Infinite	106
26	Prayer for Divine Intrusion	111
27	Messages about Love	113
28	The Water of Life in Uganda	115
29	Tipping the Scales in Favor of Hope	122
30	Where Are We? It All Depends	128
31	The Virtue of Slowing Down	135
32	Eucharist: Gathering, Listening, Loving	140
33	Life as Mystery	145
34	A Few Faces of Mary	150
35	Devotion to the Sacred Heart: What Does It Look Like Today?	154
	Index	159

Introduction

Letter writing is a venerable tradition among the leaders of many religious congregations. Saint Julie Billiart, the foundress of the Sisters of Notre Dame de Namur, wrote over 450 letters to her sisters during her years as mother superior from 1804 to 1816. My own branch of the Sisters of Notre Dame was founded in Coesfeld, Germany, in 1850. Following in the footsteps of Saint Julie, the sisters who served in leadership both on the congregational level and the provincial level wrote letters to their sisters who were often scattered across a wide geographic area. In these letters, they not only communicated news about the congregation, but more importantly, they shared insights and raised questions about the deeper aspects of the spiritual life.

This book is based on the letters I wrote to my sisters during my six years as provincial of the Chardon province of the Sisters of Notre Dame.* Though these letters were addressed principally to women living the vows of consecrated life, they have been edited to helpful to anyone striving to live the gospel. Regardless of our state in life or our gender, we are all dealing with similar challenges: trying to pray, building community, coping with change and loss, facing adversity, living our sexuality, working for greater social justice, balancing work and leisure, retaining a sense of humor, and being bearers of hope in a world often filled with violence, cynicism, and despair.

The title of each chapter reflects its theme. Because the chapters cover a wide range of topics, an index is provided at the end of the book to help you find the topics you are most interested in. Embedded within each chapter or at the end are questions that can be used for personal reflection as well as communal sharing.

In preparing this book, I owe much gratitude to several individuals. First, I want to thank the sisters in my province whose positive response to these letters gave me the impetus to publish them in book form. I also want to thank my province for giving me time to work on this book and other writing projects. And thirdly, I want to thank Sister Lenette Marcello, my personal secretary during my years as provincial, who painstakingly gathered all these letters for me. She was assisted in this endeavor by Sister Julie Rose Keck and Sister Elizabeth Wood. I could not have completed this book without the generosity of these three wonderful sisters.

Finally, a word about the title of this book. As I looked for an underlying theme in these chapters, I decided that theme was love. After all, it was love that drew me to religious life in the first place when, at age eighteen, I entered the Sisters of Notre Dame to join a group of women dedicated to making the world a better place. Years later love allowed me to say "yes" to the call to congregational leadership, despite my fears and feelings of inadequacy. That same love moved me to write these letters to my sisters in order to encourage them (as well as myself!) in our endeavor to live our faith commitment with greater enthusiasm and joy.

When God appeared to Moses and gave him the Ten Commandments for the second time, God revealed to Moses God's identity: "a God merciful and gracious, slow to anger, and abounding in steadfast love" (Ex 34:6). I love that word "steadfast." To me it connotes loyalty, faithfulness, perseverance, constancy. Our Christian faith is steadfast not because we are so strong or good or wonderful, but because it is anchored in the steadfast love of God, who cares for us more than we can imagine. It is my hope that this book, in some small way, may deepen our faith in the steadfastness of God's love.

* The Chardon province of the Sisters of Notre Dame is one of fifteen provinces of a large international congregation, a congregation with more than 2,300 sisters serving in fifteen different countries. For more information about our congregation you can visit these two Web sites: www.snd1.org or www.sndchardon.org.

CHAPTER 1

Abounding in Steadfast Love

Several years ago I visited an old friend, Father Demetrius Dumm, a Benedictine from St. Vincent Archabbey in Latrobe, Pennsylvania. He was working on another book, this time on the Gospel of John. We were talking about the fact that in John's account of the Last Supper, there is no mention of the institution of the Eucharist. Demetrius said that John takes the institution of the Eucharist from the Last Supper and places it with the discourse on the Bread of Life in chapter six. At the Last Supper, John puts in its place the washing of the feet. Demetrius called the washing of the feet a "eucharistic act," that is, an act of selfless loving. By substituting the institution of the Eucharist with the washing of the feet, John seems to be saying, among other things, that the celebration of the Eucharist must never be separated from concrete acts of selfless giving.

We are all familiar with John's beautiful description of the washing of the feet. The gospel tells how Jesus got up from the table, removed his outer garment, and, taking a towel, wrapped it around his waist. He then poured water into a basin and began to wash the disciples' feet and to wipe them with the towel he was wearing (Jn 13:4–5).

Jesus tied a towel around his waist, turning the towel into a makeshift apron, and washed the feet of his disciples. One theologian offered the following suggestion. He noted that when a man is consecrated bishop, he is given a crosier, a symbol of the Good Shepherd, a beautiful image of leadership. But in addition to the crosier, maybe every bishop should be given an apron as a symbol of his call to serve others selflessly, as Jesus did.

When I became provincial, I gave each sister on my leadership team an apron. I asked that every time she tied this apron around her waist, she would recall Jesus tying the towel around his waist at the Last Supper. I hoped that the apron would be a reminder to her that saying "yes" to the service of leadership was truly a eucharistic act, an act of selfless giving.

Strengthening Community

Community is integral to our lives as Christians and as religious. There are several ways we can strengthen community. The first is this: Let us assume the good will of one another. A brief story illustrates this point. One day a man was driving his new red sports car down a country road. As he was about to round a curve, he suddenly saw a car careening out of control and coming straight at him. The driver, a woman, swerved back just in time to avoid him. As she passed, she shouted at him, "Pig!" The man angrily shouted back at her, "Cow!" He felt good that he had yelled at her before she got away. Then he sped around the curve and ran into a pig.

The man had assumed ill will on the woman's part. He had assumed she was calling him a pig! But the woman was actually warning him of danger on the road ahead. He had misjudged her, responded angrily, and had an accident. Maybe we can recall this story the next time we are quick to judge the actions or words of another.

The second way we can strengthen community is this: Let us be patient with one another. The following is a story from the book *Holy Folly: Short and Tall Tales from the Abbey of Gethsemane.* Brother Matthew at Gethsemane was in charge of maintenance. Every now and then he had to post a note to inform the community of some problem. He would write a note that a toilet was broken or the water was going to be turned off or the main stairs were closed for repair. Here is one of his notes.

New Patrons,

Welcome to our facility! If you shower with the curtains inside the tub, the water will not get all over the floor. If it does run over, please mop it up. The high pressure water line runs the length of this corridor. It makes much noise. So showering after bedtime will not win you friends and may lose you some.

Until we have a better world,

Brother Matthew

Until we have a better world. I like that! If only we would be more patient with the world we have and with the humans who inhabit it. If only we would be more understanding, more forgiving, more compassionate. Jesus was. We know how patient he was when we catch glimpses of him ready to lose his patience–especially with his disciples. We hear him say things like this. To Philip: "Have I been with you so long and you still don't know who I am?" To Peter, "Get behind me, Satan!" And to the Pharisees: "You hypocrites!"

Jesus fully embraced the human condition with its pettiness and limitations. He believed that the Spirit was active and alive despite our human frailties. He believed that people could change for the better. He believed that the ultimate reality was not death but life; not evil but goodness. But patience is not an easy virtue for many of us today. Someone has noted that, in the old days, if a person missed the stagecoach, he was content to wait a day or two for the next one. Nowadays, we become frustrated if we miss one section of a revolving door. We can begin to strengthen community, then, by our patient acceptance of our human limitations.

A third way we strengthen community is by *seeking the truth together.* When I became provincial I asked the sisters to be honest with me and with our leadership team. By doing so, I was inviting feedback—both negative and positive—because I knew we would need the community's honesty to serve them well. We as a leadership team, in turn, had to be honest with our members in our quest for truth. But truth is always bigger than my opinion or your opinion. Truth starts there but goes further. My truth has to be open to your truth. Your truth must be open to mine. Also, as we all know, the truth is not always easy to hear. It's not always pleasant. As someone once remarked, "The truth can ouch."

A president of a large university was asked to name some qualities essential for a good leader. Instantly he said, "The ability to inflict pain." Good leaders do not try to make people miserable, but they sometimes ask people to do hard things. Good leaders show love and compassion, yes, but they also challenge. Some leaders challenge us to accept difficult ministries, to re-evaluate our choices, to reassess the direction we are going in. Such challenges can be painful. I did not look forward to the pain and darkness that would be a part of my term as provincial. But I firmly believed that God would be present amid the pain and darkness, saying to us, "I am with you, even in this!"

When I became provincial, some people asked about my vision for the future. I said I didn't have a clear vision of our future, but I was eager to pursue the vision with all of them. In her book, Spiritlinking Leadership, Sister Donna Markham says, good leaders "learn to navigate in the fog." They have a sense of direction, yes, but not necessarily a clear vision of the destination. As provincial, I looked forward to navigating in the fog with the sisters, to setting the course with them, to discerning the right direction with them.

Another way we strengthen community is by hoping together. It's hard to be hopeful in today's world. That's one reason we find so much cynicism. The writer Rich Heffern has defined cynicism as "the voice that says no better world is possible." Such an attitude is diametrically opposed to the life and teachings of Jesus. We cannot be Christians and cynics at the same time. These two stances are incompatible. Yet who of us is completely free of the tyranny of cynicism? It's in the very air we breathe. We know we are succumbing to cynicism when we find ourselves saying things such as, "What's the use?…It won't work…Been there, done that…Same old, same old…Things just keep getting worse."

A wise person said, "A cynic is someone who is prematurely disappointed in the future." We should regularly ask ourselves, what is my attitude toward the future? We want to be people rooted in the real world, yes, and the real world is not always a safe, comfortable, or logical place. The real world can inflict pain—unspeakable pain. When this happens, the temptation is to withdraw, pull back, close down. But we can't afford to do this. Why? Because only in the real world do we encounter the living God. Only in the real world is salvation possible.

So then, let us don our aprons together and serve selflessly. Let us explore ways of strengthening community. Let us pursue the vision of a better future together. And let us hope together, remembering that our hope is rooted not in our own strength but in our God who is "merciful and gracious, slow to anger, and abounding in steadfast love" (Ex 34:6).

❧ *What is my attitude toward the future? Is it fearful or cynical? Or is it hopeful and expectant?*

CHAPTER 2

Notes and Poems from India

In October of 1949, six Sisters of Notre Dame from the Chardon province set sail for Patna, India, to begin a new mission there. Today there are over 250 Sisters of Notre Dame in India, serving in schools, parishes, clinics, retreat centers, social agencies, and other settings. On Monday, October 25, 1999, I flew to India to attend the fiftieth anniversary celebration of the founding of the mission in Patna. I was accompanied by Sister Valerie Sweeney, director of the Notre Dame India Mission. What follows is a brief description of that celebration as well as a few poems that grew out of my experience in India.

Sister Valerie and I returned from our two-week trip to India. The highlight of our trip was the fiftieth Jubilee celebration of our sisters in India. On October 31, over 900 friends, colleagues, and students gathered under a red, white, and gold tent in Patna to offer a Mass of thanksgiving. Five bishops and more than sixty priests joined in the two-hour liturgical celebration in Hindi, which included beautiful music and dancing. After a delicious luncheon, we gathered in the school auditorium and watched a presentation of song, dance, and drama depicting the history of the Sisters of Notre Dame in India. Special tributes were given to the eighteen American sisters who served in India since the founding of the mission.

Visiting some of the sisters in Delhi, Patna, Bangalore, and Mysore was another highlight for us. I was impressed by the sisters' hospitality and by the good works they are doing everywhere. Experiencing firsthand the history, art, and religious faith of the Indian people was also a special privilege. Sister Valerie and I were deeply edified by the many individuals we saw at prayer in every church, mosque, shrine, and temple we entered.

Of course, we saw another side of India, too. Nothing could have prepared me for the abject poverty I experienced everywhere—the sights, sounds, and smells. Yes, we here in the United States have terrible poverty, but it doesn't begin to compare with the vastness and depth of the poverty I saw in India. I still choke up when I try to describe some of the things I witnessed in India—whole families sleeping out on the streets at night, schools with no books, Mother Teresa's home for abandoned babies in Calcutta (120 little children were there the day we came, 90 girls and 30 boys), children playing in garbage dumps, and everywhere the beggars. Before I left for India, a Jesuit friend who has been to India told me, "India will change you forever, Melannie." He was right. Although I cannot begin to articulate that change, I sense that it has taken place on a deep level inside me. Sister Valerie and I traveled more than 30,000 miles in those two weeks, but I suspect the journey inward was even longer, deeper, and more significant.

The following are a few poems I wrote while visiting India.

Crazy Questions

I wake up in the hotel room in Delhi
  and automatically go to the bathroom.
As I flush the toilet, I ask myself,
    "What are all those homeless people doing this morning
    waking up on the streets below
        —those thousands and thousands without any toilets?"
I brush my teeth and ask, "What are all those people doing
    who have no toothbrushes?"
I wash my face and ask the person in the mirror,
    "How come you—an American—
        are using the precious water of India?"

Then I dry my face with a towel and say,
    "You will drive yourself crazy with such questions. Stop it!"
But I can't stop it.
Later I think: Maybe the really crazy thing to do
    is to stop asking such questions.

The Taj Mahal

In the morning sun,
    catching our first glimpse, we gasp!
Wedding cake in stone!

The Tourist and the Rickshaw Driver

Around my waist
    is more money
    than this man makes
        in a lifetime.
Something is wrong here.
    Diabolically wrong.

My Water Bottle

Everywhere I go,
    I carry my water bottle,
        irrefutable proof
        of my inability
            —despite the sari I wear—
        to enter fully
    into their world.

"Life Is Not Fair"

"Life is not fair!" we cry when we feel cheated or robbed
   of something we assume to be rightfully ours.
But here in India,
   amid the filth and squalor,
   I find myself crying, "Life is not fair!"—
      not in outrage,
      but in profound, personal shame.

Sister Sudha, SND, Lawyer

A soft spoken woman
   in a red sari,
      she labors for women's rights
         among the poorest of the poor,
         rape cases and land disputes
            her specialty.
When I ask her why
   she does what she does
   despite the danger,
      she says:
         "Years ago
         I decided to give my life
         for those who deserve it the most."
She does.
They do.

Misery

Everywhere I look
  misery.
I cry out,
  "I'm sorry you have to live like this!
But it's not my fault!
I'm not to blame!
It's partly your own fault!
  If only you would work harder,
    get an education,
    elect honest officials,
    be more responsible!"
Yet, in my heart I know
  they aren't really to blame.
Nor am I really innocent.

❧ *What struck me the most in this chapter?*

CHAPTER 3

Higher, Higher! More, More!

Years ago I was pushing my little niece on the swing in her backyard. "Higher, higher," she kept yelling to me. After a while my arms began to ache, so I said, "I have to stop now, Melissa." But she yelled back, "No, Auntie! I want more, more!"

Higher, higher! More, more! My niece's words express the primeval cry of all human beings, don't they? As humans, we are never satisfied. Enough is not enough. We always seek more. Saint Augustine said it best: "Our hearts are restless, Lord, until they rest in thee." I sometimes call this innate restlessness our holy hunger for the more. I firmly believe that restlessness is central to our lives. Total fulfillment is always beyond our reach. As Father Michael Himes of Boston College said somewhat facetiously, "If you want to see a totally fulfilled human being, drop into your local cemetery." I also believe that befriending this restlessness, this hunger for more, rather than denying it or running away from it, is one of the most important decisions we can make in life.

Befriending our innate hunger for more is not easy. For one thing, our society tells us that complete satisfaction is possible in this life. It says things like this: Buy this car, wear these clothes, drink this brand of beer, land this job, befriend the right people, achieve this certain goal, and you will reach fulfillment. As Christians and as religious we know, of course, that this is not true, and yet sometimes even we buy into this illusion. When we experience hunger or restlessness, do we automatically conclude that something is wrong? Do we immediately seek a change—a change in ministry, local community, friends, spiritual director, or even vocation? Or can we sit with our hunger for a while, enduring its ache and emptiness, realizing it voices a truth we cannot afford to miss. That truth is this: We do not make sense all by ourselves. We do not make sense even in relationship with another. We do not make sense even in a community. No, we make sense only when we are united to God, the "home" toward which we are journeying.

> ❧ *How have I experienced this holy hunger for the more? What can help me to befriend it and endure its ache and emptiness?*

Consecrated religious pronounce three vows of chastity, poverty, and obedience. We can look at the three vows in light of this restlessness and holy hunger. By the vow of chastity, for instance, religious vow to remain unmarried. More concretely, they vow a bunch of "not's": not to engage in sex, not to enter into any exclusive relationship with another human being, not to have children. Talk about denial! For most people, being someone's lover and/or being someone's parent are the ordinary means toward human fulfillment. Yet, religious deny themselves of these legitimate, good, healthy, and holy realities. What a tremendous sacrifice they make! I, for one, experience this sacrifice of my chastity every time I hold a newborn baby, spot a middle-aged couple holding hands, or have to say farewell to a good friend. Why, then, do religious make the vow of chastity? Why do they choose such an apparently inhuman thing? The Constitutions of my congregation express it well: "By our life of chastity for the sake of the kingdom of heaven, we witness to our union with Christ which will be fulfilled in the life to come" (article 18). The key phrase here is "union with Christ." Consecrated chastity for any other motive makes little sense; it misses the mark. But notice, even this union is not fulfilled in this life but in "the life to come."

> ❧ *If I am a religious, how do I live the sacrifices inherent in my vow of chastity? What are some ways I nourish my union with Christ?*

The vow of poverty speaks eloquently of holy hunger. Why do religious renounce the ownership of property? Why do they seek to identify themselves with the poor? They do so because the reality is that they are poor. As humans, they are limited. They are ultimately dependent. By taking the vow of poverty they publicly proclaim this fact. In other words, they publicly embrace the human condition of contingency. The Constitutions of my Congregation tell us that "we are pilgrim people who have here no lasting city but look with hope to the one that is to come" (article 29). The greatest threat to the vow of poverty, then, is not having too many things. Rather it is forsaking the journey. It is settling down. It is staying put or—worse yet—turning back when the journey becomes difficult—and it will!

   ✦ *Have I even been tempted to give up the journey, to settle down,*
     to stay put, or to turn back? What keeps me from giving in to
     this temptation?

Obedience, too, witnesses to restlessness and hunger for more. By obedience religious vow to listen. Why? Because they do not have all the answers. What do they vow to listen to? They vow to listen to their inner movements, to the daily circumstances of their particular lives, to their God in prayer, to the larger world in which they live, to the cry of the poor, to the teachings of the Church, and to the group of women with whom they have cast their lot in life. Through obedience, they promise not to go it alone, but to journey in community—in my case the community is the Sisters of Notre Dame. Religious promise not to rely solely on their own judgment, insights, and talents, but to lay them all before the community for appraisal. They promise to offer their appraisal of their sisters' judgments, insights, and talents. Obedience is not easy. The Constitutions remind them that often their obedience, "like Mary's fiat, will be a surrender of love made in faith, leading through darkness to light" (article 37).

   ✦ *What judgments, insights, and talents have I laid before others*
     recently? How have I offered my appraisal of the judgments,
     insights, and talents of others?

Jesus spoke often about this holy hunger for the more. Perhaps one of his most explicit expressions was the fourth beatitude: "Blessed are you who are hungry now, for you will be filled" (Lk 6:21). This holy hunger can take many forms: loneliness, anxiety, jealousy, bereavement, boredom, feelings of inadequacy. Henri Nouwen, always a realist, said this about restlessness: "To wait for moments or places where no pain exists, no separation is felt and where all human restlessness has turned to inner peace is waiting for a dream world. No (one)...will be able to rest our deepest craving for unity and wholeness." Sometimes the hunger we experience is, in Sebastian Moore's words, "The desire for I know not what." We hunger not for this or that particular thing, but for the "un-nameable."

At certain times in our lives the hunger is more intense than at other times. Midlife, for example, is notorious for arousing restlessness and hunger. Sometimes these longings become even more pronounced in our final years, when the limitations in body and mind become more real. But restlessness and holy hunger can arise at any time. Even when everything in our life is going well, we can still hear a little voice inside crying, "More, more!"

Amid all this, we remember that sometimes our restlessness is, in fact, urging us to do something, to change something, perhaps our attitudes, our priorities, or our expectations. It can be calling us to alter our behavior or to finally accept the fact that we will never have a better past. How do we tell the difference between the restlessness we must embrace and the restlessness urging us to action? Only through careful, prayerful discernment.

Many spiritual authors have written eloquently on this theme of hunger and restlessness. Rabbi Abraham Heschel wrote, "(The one) who is satisfied has never truly craved....Contentment is the shadow not the light." Someone said of Thomas Merton, "He was constantly restless, as all great searchers are." And Gary Wills wrote of Dorothy Day's "moral discontent." He said, "She reposed in restlessness."

The Indian poet Rabindranath Tagore has written a beautiful poem on restlessness and hunger. Addressing God, he says:

If it is not my portion to meet thee in this life,
then let me ever feel that I have missed thy sight....
As my days pass in the crowded market of this world
and my hands grow full with the daily profits,
let me ever feel that I have gained nothing....
When I sit by the roadside, tired and panting,
when I spread my bed low in the dust,
let me ever feel that the long journey is still before me.

RABINDRANATH TAGORE, *Gitanjali*

As we journey through life, may we grow in our hunger to meet Jesus. May we always feel as if we have so much more to gain. May we always feel that the journey is still before us. May we always hear, in the "more, more" of our hearts, our good God calling us home!

CHAPTER 4

Mary's Annunciation

In one of his poems, Gerard Manley Hopkins compares Mary to the air we breathe. He says to her: "Be thou then, O thou dear/ Mother, my atmosphere." The image is more than a quaint expression from a bygone piety. It is a powerful metaphor that underscores Mary's persuasive influence upon our 2,000-year-old Christian history. But what about our own personal history? What influence does Mary have on our lives as Christians? What insights can we glean from her words and example—especially on this beautiful feast of the Annunciation? Let us reflect on four insights in particular.

First of all, the Annunciation reminds us that we encounter God in the real world. Mary lived in a particular time (during the reign of Caesar Augustus) and in a particular place (Nazareth in Galilee). She lived in the real world of hunger, sweat, tears, laughter, loving relationships, fatigue, joy, political unrest, beautiful sunsets, violence, and injustice of all kinds. Like us, Mary could be in only one place at a time, she was limited in what she could do with her life, and she didn't know what the future held. The fact that Mary lived in a real time and place both consoles and challenges us. It consoles us because it reminds us that God is, indeed, active and alive in our historical time period and in our geographical place. It challenges us for it makes us ask can we, like Mary, welcome God into the particular circumstances of our lives? Can we, if necessary, readjust or radically alter our own plans in favor of God's plan?

The feast of the Annunciation reminds us that Mary was troubled at times. When the angel Gabriel appeared to Mary and said: "Greetings, favored one! The Lord is with you," what was Mary's response? Luke tells us "she was much perplexed by [the angel's] words" (Lk 1:28–29). Mary wasn't merely annoyed or mildly disturbed. No, she was much perplexed or, as another translation says, she was "greatly troubled." Why? For one thing, Mary didn't know what was happening. She didn't have a script to tell her what to do or say. There was no heavenly director telling her, "Now, Mary, you kneel over there and when Gabriel comes in, look surprised!" No, Mary had to ad lib her life—just as we do. Like Mary, we, too, know times when we are greatly troubled. Perhaps we have to give up a cherished ministry, work with a difficult person, or face serious illness. Or maybe we feel greatly troubled as we helplessly watch the diminishment of our numbers or the dying of a loved one. The Annunciation tells us that life doesn't always make sense. But Mary did not expect life to make sense all the time. Instead she expected something better: that God would be with her everywhere and always, even amid life's apparent absurdities. Can we also trust that God is at work in all the events of our lives—or only in the ones that meet our expectations or approval?

Mary pondered. When Gabriel greeted Mary at the Annunciation, Mary "pondered what sort of greeting this might be." It is interesting to note that the word "ponder" is etymologically related to the word "pendulum." A pendulum is something that swings freely back and forth. To ponder, then, means to go back and forth freely before choosing or deciding. The word implies that Mary weighed things carefully, that she thought things over, that she did not jump to conclusions. In other words, Mary was patient with ambiguity. She tolerated inconclusiveness. She was able to endure uncertainty. What about us? Do we ponder things carefully, or do we immediately jump to conclusions? Can we be patient with a certain amount of ambiguity in our lives or must we always demand absolute clarity?

The fourth insight we can glean from the feast is that Mary served others. Mary's fiat resulted in a radical change in her life and her person. By saying "yes," Mary welcomed the intrusion of another human being into her very body and life. Such selflessness! Such daring! Similarly,

Mary's first action after the Annunciation was another act of immense generosity: she scurried over the hills to assist her cousin Elizabeth who was also with child. The Annunciation reminds us that service is the natural outflow of any encounter with God. Paradoxically, service is also the preparatory work for any encounter with God. Recently, a young man asked his local bishop what books he should read to get to know God better. The bishop replied, "No books. Go out and serve the poor in our city." How does our prayer lead to service? How does our service lead us to God?

When celebrating a feast such as the Annunciation, there is a tendency to look backward and to focus only on Mary. But this feast calls us to look at our own lives in the present and for the future. Mary spoke her fiat over 2,000 years ago poised before a future filled with both uncertainty and possibility. Her fiat is not about acquiescence and passivity. It is about daring and empowerment. She who had found favor with God said "yes" to God's wild plan of salvation. We might ask ourselves: What is God asking of me at this particular time in my life? What am I being asked to say fiat to?

Fifty years ago the writer Caryll Houselander said this of Mary: "We shall not be asked to do more than the Mother of God....What we shall be asked to give is our flesh and blood, our daily life....To surrender all that we are, as we are, to the Spirit of Love in order that our lives may bear Christ into the world." On this beautiful feast of the Annunciation, my prayer for all of us is that, like Mary, we may dare to surrender all that we are to the empowering Spirit of Love.

❧ *To what extent is Mary's experience like my experience?*

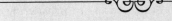

CHAPTER 5

Fear and Peace at Easter

As I was reading the account of the first Easter a few days ago, these two words jumped out at me: fear and peace. In this reflection we will look briefly at the role of fear and peace in the Resurrection story and in our spiritual life.

Scholars tell us that the Gospel of Mark is probably the oldest gospel. In eight short verses, Mark presents the story of the resurrection. Early Sunday morning, three women are on their way to the tomb to anoint Jesus' body. As they walk along together, they ask themselves, "Who will roll back the stone for us?" for the stone was very large. When they arrive at the tomb, they discover, much to their surprise, that the stone has already been rolled back. Peering cautiously into the tomb, they see an angel robed in white. They are "utterly amazed." The angel tells them not to be afraid, for Jesus has been raised from the dead. The angel directs them to go and tell the disciples the good news, assuring them they will see Jesus again in Galilee. Chapter 16, verse 8, the last verse of the original gospel, is this: "So they went out and fled from the tomb, for terror and amazement had seized them; and they said nothing to anyone, for they were afraid."

Notice these words: they fled from the tomb…terror and amazement had seized them…they were afraid. Mark's original gospel ends, not with three women dancing around singing alleluias, but with three women running away from an empty tomb, scared out of their wits! And who can blame them? For the totally unexpected has happened. Jesus is risen!

The impossible has become a reality. Jesus is risen! The too-good-to-be-true is true. Jesus is risen! With the news of Jesus' resurrection, the women realize instantly and rightly that nothing is ever going to be the same again. Their initial response to such an earth-shattering event is not a shallow, "How nice!" but a terrified, "My God! Now what?"

Easter reminds us that fear has a rightful place in our spiritual lives. Why should we, in one sense, fear even God? Because God is totally other. In his book The Trivialization of God, Donald McCullough says God is "wholly other, radically different from anything else in creation, terrifying in greatness." McCullough's words echo those of Saint Augustine who wrote, "It is easier for us to say what God is not, than what God is." A healthy fear of God means we never, in the name of love or anything else, reduce God to some sort of cosmic chum or divine bellboy. We never equate God's will with our personal preferences. No, God is God, and we are we. And the difference between us is inexpressible. Jesus, of course, came to span that chasm. By revealing God's great love for us, Jesus helps us move in the direction of greater trust in God, in Abba. Still, the fact remains, a profound reverence for God will always be a necessary component of a loving relationship with God.

Easter reminds us of something else we have to fear: evil. In fact Easter Sunday is so incredibly wonderful precisely because Good Friday was so incredibly awful. Easter warns us to take evil seriously. It tells us to never underestimate evil's power. All we have to do is to look around us, and we see clear signs of evil's potency. For example, six out of every ten people in the world live in shanty towns; one in every five Americans is functionally illiterate; the three richest people in the world have assets that exceed the combined gross national product of the forty-eight least-developed countries; more than 200,000 children under eighteen serve in armies worldwide; 1.2 million babies in the world have AIDS; the only western democracy that still has the death penalty is the United States. The Easter story does not downplay evil. Rather, it promises us that evil does not have the last word. Goodness does, and one way goodness is brought to birth is by our selfless loving. We might ask ourselves:

How seriously do I take evil? How am I bringing goodness to birth by my selfless loving?

The second Easter word is peace. "Peace be with you," says Jesus to his terrified disciples after the Resurrection. We who claim to be disciples of Jesus are called to bring peace to others just as Jesus did. In his book *Touching the Holy*, Robert Wicks tells of seeing two contrasting tombstones in a cemetery. One was the large imposing marker of a deceased general, which listed all his battles and accomplishments. The other was a small stone marking the grave of a young woman who had died at the age of twenty-one. Her husband's inscription read simply: "Everywhere she went, she brought flowers." Easter is a good time to remind ourselves that when we die, we do not take with us anything we have earned or accomplished. We take with us only who we have become. We might ask ourselves: Am I becoming a person of peace?

We become women and men of peace by being more aware of the little ways we do violence every day. Thomas Merton said that when he undertook to embrace a life of nonviolence, he started by closing doors softly. Perhaps we can start with that small gesture and move on to other gestures such as walking more slowly, driving less frantically, speaking more respectfully to and about others, letting someone else go ahead of us in line, doing with less "stuff," spending time with an elderly person.

Sister Joan Chittister says this about peace: "Peace comes from not needing to control everything, not needing to have everything." Two words: fear and peace. Both lie at the heart of the Easter narrative and of our spiritual lives. My Easter prayer for all of us is a simple one: May our legitimate fears drive us into the arms of our almighty and all-loving God. May we take evil seriously, responding with the goodness born of our selfless loving. And may we become true Easter people, bringing the flowers of peace wherever we softly tread.

CHAPTER 6

Prayer of Thanksgiving for All the Seasons of Our Lives

Eternal God, Timeless One,
   you tell us: "For everything there is a season, and
   a time for every matter under heaven" (Eccl 3:1).
We thank you for the seasons of our lives,
   for the gift of these times:
   A time to be born and a time to die.
   A time to weep and a time to laugh.
   A time to scatter stones and a time to gather them.
   A time to do and a time to be done to.
   A time to stay, a time to leave,
      and a time to meet in the middle again.
   A time to say hello, a time to say goodbye,
      and a time to say hello again.
   A time to say yes, a time to say no,
      and a time where yes is no and no is yes.
   A time to be young and a time to be older.
   A time to hold on to and a time to let go of.

A time to follow, a time to lead,
and a time when no one remembers who's following or leading.
A time to toe the line and a time to break the rules.
A time to plant, a time to uproot,
and a time to plant the seeds of what was uprooted.
A time to celebrate, a time to mourn,
and a time to celebrate with no mourning after.
A time to say, "I'm sorry" and a time to say, "I forgive."
A time to ask, "What if?" and a time to bless what is.
A time to be hurt, a time to be healed, a time to be held,
and a time to simply behold.
Eternal One, O Timeless One,
we thank you for all the seasons of our lives,
for the gift of these times
but especially for today. Amen.

❧ *What lines in this reflection resonate with where I am now?*

CHAPTER 7

"One Wild and Precious Life"

The poet Mary Oliver has written a beautiful poem entitled "The Summer Day." The last two lines pose this question: "Tell me, what is it you plan to do/ With your one wild and precious life?

Oliver's question is a very fitting question for the feast of Pentecost. For Pentecost marks that dramatic moment when the first disciples, newly intoxicated with the Holy Spirit, decide what to do with the rest of their lives. These three words of Oliver can offer new insights into this feast: one, wild, and precious.

One. What strikes me first about the story of Pentecost is the fact that the Holy Spirit came when the disciples "were all together in one place" (Acts 2:1). Why were they gathered together? Because Jesus told them to. At the Ascension, he directed the disciples to return to Jerusalem and wait for the coming of the Spirit—together. And while they were doing that, the Spirit came. The Pentecost event, then, is rooted in community. Writer Kathleen Norris in her book *Amazing Grace* says it well: "Christianity…is inescapably communal." Like those disciples at Pentecost, we Christians today are gathered in Jesus' name. Pentecost is a fitting time for us to celebrate our common discipleship. It is a time to remember that the essence of our oneness is not a common church building, not a shared neighborhood, not even similar tastes. No, the essence of our oneness is our common call and our common response to the person of Jesus.

❧ *What are some ways we celebrate our common discipleship?*

What also impresses me about the first Pentecost is how the disciples were gathered together. What were they doing in that upper room while they were waiting for the Spirit? Scripture tells us they were praying together. This means they were probably singing psalms together. They were probably sharing their personal experience of Jesus, how they had first met Jesus, what he said to them, how he had radically changed their lives. Perhaps they were also sharing their dreams and hopes, their fears and doubts. But it is not too far-fetched to imagine that most of the disciples were very afraid. Perhaps some gave up hope and even left the upper room before the Spirit came. The point is, the disciples who gathered together in that upper room were very much like us: fearful, uncertain, and painfully in touch with their human weakness. Isn't that consoling? The Holy Spirit did not descend upon the disciples when they were confident, sure, and strong, but when they were vulnerable and most in need. Someone has said, "The real Christian is one who can praise God from the ruins of life." Pentecost reminds us that the Spirit of God can break into our lives both individually and communally, at any moment, even when our lives are unraveling or falling apart.

❧ *Have we—individually and/or communally—ever praised God from the ruins of life?*

The second word we will reflect on is the word "wild." The first Pentecost was, indeed, a wild event. The winds howled, the walls rattled, the ground shook. Clearly, the Holy Spirit came not as a gentle breeze, but as a hurricane and earthquake. It was as if God were trying to impress upon the disciples (and upon us!) that God's Spirit will not be controlled. It will not be tamed. Pentecost is a good time to ask ourselves, do we ever try to control or tame God's Spirit? We do this when we find ourselves thinking things like this: "If I pray hard and long enough, God will give me what I'm asking for." Or, "If I am faithful to Christ, he will not let anything bad happen to me or my loved ones." Or, "I've given God so many years. Now I can settle down and take it easy." Or do we, like those early disciples, allow God's Spirit full reign in our lives? Do we allow our lives to be blown open by divine love?

When we celebrate the sacraments, that's exactly what we are doing. In baptism, in confirmation, in the Eucharist, in reconciliation, we are doing a wildly Pentecostal thing by allowing our lives to be blown open by the Spirit. By following Christ we have proclaimed that God is worthy of the total gift of self, the unrestrained donation of our complete person. Lived authentically, our baptismal commitment will bring us face to face with a God who is not only in the whirlwind but who is the whirlwind. If we live our baptismal vows faithfully, they will bring us face to face also with others, who will test our good intentions, unsettle our complacency, and call forth our compassion. Following Christ faithfully will bring us face to face with self, which is sometimes the most difficult encounter of all! In short, baptism and the other sacraments are Pentecostal when they continuously call us to ever greater loving.

❦ *How does living my commitment to Christ bring me face to face with God, with others, with self? Are my baptismal vows calling me to ever greater loving?*

The third word for Pentecost is the word "precious." While I was provincial, three sisters of my community all died on the same day. We were stunned. In the midst of our grieving, someone asked me, "What do you think God is trying to tell us?" I said, "God is trying to tell us what God is always trying to tell us—at every Eucharist, with every Scripture reading, in our own personal prayer. God is telling us: Life is a gift, life is precious, love one another, allow others to love you, take up your cross, follow me, trust me." The death of any person calls us to gratitude for the precious gift of life. It invites us to open ourselves more and more to the life-giving Spirit of God.

The most important action of Pentecost was the sending forth of the disciples from that upper room. The disciples were almost catapulted out into the streets, so on fire were they with the power of the Spirit. So great was their joy and enthusiasm that many bystanders thought they were drunk. So persuasive was their speech, that 3,000 were converted to the gospel in that single day. Some homily! Pentecost makes it clear:

the coming of God's Spirit is a demanding thing. It demands that we become new people, we see with new eyes, we speak with new tongues, and we choose with new hearts. The coming of the Spirit connects us to everything, to everyone. It demands that we carry in our hearts the sufferings of the ill, the joys of the jubilant, the dreams of children, the hunger for peace and justice of all.

❧ *How do my actions show my conviction that life is a precious gift? What do I carry in my heart?*

In her poem, Mary Oliver asks the question, "What is it you plan to do?" Her question reminds us that life doesn't just happen. To a large extent, we influence the course our life takes—if not by our choices, then at least by our attitudes. Pentecost tells us that grace happens. It happens because the Holy Spirit lives in us. Pentecost also tells us that faith is essentially forward looking. The disciples left the upper room where they were dwelling upon the past. They went forth from that upper room to radically influence the future by their proclamation of the gospel.

The Spirit is calling us to move forward too. The Spirit calls us to radically influence our future. To this end, my prayer for all of us is a simple one: "Come, Holy Spirit, come! Make us one! Fill us with your wild wisdom! Fill us with your precious love!"

CHAPTER 8

The God Who Calls

God calls. Scripture is replete with examples of individuals who were called by God: Abraham, Moses, Gideon, Judith, Esther, Jeremiah, Isaiah, Mary—to name but a few. God calls. We know this truth not only from Scripture, but also from our own lived experience. Did not each one of us hear a call from God that brought us to the Christian faith? Within our current circumstances, do we not continue to hear God's call directing our decisions? God calls in many creative ways. No two calls from God are identical. Yet, when we reflect on our own call and on God's call in Scripture, we detect certain similarities or common threads. Let us focus in on six of these threads.

God takes the initiative in calling us. Scripture is clear. God takes the initiative in calling us. Abraham was enjoying his "golden years" when God called him to go to "the land that I will show you" (Gen 12:1). Moses was minding his own business—namely, herding sheep—when God called him to lead the Israelites out of Egypt (Ex 3-4). Gideon was threshing wheat in the wine press when God called him to deliver his people from the Midianites (Jgs 6). The fact that God takes the initiative in calling us, in establishing a relationship with us, is immensely consoling. It means that God is more eager to know us than we could ever be to know God. Even if we try to run away from God, we cannot. God will pursue us relentlessly. Francis Thompson's classic poem "The Hound of Heaven" reverberates with this theme.

I fled Him, down the nights and down the days;
I fled Him, down the arches of the years;
I fled Him, down the labyrinthine ways
Of my own mind.

❧ *As someone has wisely said, "Summoned or not, God comes."*
Have I ever experienced God as relentless pursuer?

God's call is always incarnational. God's call is never abstract. It never merely stays inside our head. Rather, God's call is incarnational. It affects our everyday lives. Perhaps the word "affects" is not strong enough. It might be more accurate to say that often God's call disrupts our lives, interferes with our plans, messes up our agenda. God's call does not affect just our own lives either. It impacts the lives of others— our family, friends, religious community, church, country, and even world. When Abraham said "yes" to God and left his homeland, he and his entire family embarked on a journey that zigzagged back and forth across Mesopotamia, Assyria, Egypt, the Sinai Peninsula, and Canaan. How much more incarnational can you get? When Mary said "yes" to God, her relationship with Joseph radically changed. So too, our "yes" to God's call will be incarnational, that is, it will determine where we live, how we relate to people, and what we do with our time.

❧ *In what ways is God's call to me incarnational? Has my life*
journey ever zigzagged? How has my "yes" to God affected other
people in my life?

God calls us to serve others. When God called Abraham, Moses, and Mary, God asked them to do something. God gave them a mission. So too, when God calls us, God invites us to do something, and that something always involves loving others. In one sense we can say God's call is always an invitation to greater selflessness. I was reminded of this one day in my sixth month as provincial when, feeling frustrated, I wrote in my journal, "My life is not my own!!!" Those words were part of my complaint to God. Later, I was able to smile at those words, and say: "Of course my life is not my own! My life doesn't belong to me. It belongs to God—by birth, by baptism, by religious vows. My life belongs to others too—my family, my sisters in community, my colleagues, the people to whom I minister. My life especially belongs to those who are poor and needy. I did not become a religious sister to hoard my life. I came to give it away. I came not to 'nest.' I came to serve—not just for ten years or forty years or even for sixty-five years—but for my whole life. The word "whole" refers not merely to the length of my years, but, more importantly, to the quality of my loving.

To whom does my life belong? Prove it!

God accompanies the one who is called. God does not call us to do something, and then God walks away. No, God accompanies us on our mission every step of the way, even during times of pain and darkness. Saint Julie Billiart certainly believed this and lived it. Over and over again in her letters she reminds her sisters to trust in God's unfailing presence in their lives. She writes, "The Good God will not leave us on our road without giving us light and grace to guide us" (letter 260). When Julie was ordered to leave Amiens by the bishop of the diocese, she at first cried a lot. But when the actual day came for her departure to Namur, "she accepted the dismissal in peace" (*Julie Billiart: Woman of Courage*, Roseanne Murphy, SNDdeN). Why? Because Julie knew that God would be with her in Namur just as God had been with her in Amiens. As the great theologian Karl Rahner, SJ, said, "We have no choice. God is with us."

❧ *Have I experienced God's presence? What did it feel like? Have I experienced God's "absence"? What did it feel like?*

God's call is repeated again and again. God never calls us "once and for all." We cannot say, "I answered God's call once. Now I can rest." No, God calls us again and again. When Sister Maria Aloysia Wolbring pronounced her vows in Coesfeld, Germany, she probably never realized that her "yes" to God would lead to another "yes" to leave her homeland and journey to Cleveland, Ohio! By our baptism, we all answered God's invitation to follow Christ, but within that call lie other calls: to a particular parish community, to particular friends, to a deeper prayer life, to an acceptance of diminishment. We continuously ask ourselves, "How does God want me to live as a Christian at this time in my life? How is God asking me to give concrete expression to my Christian calling in this particular situation?"

❧ What are some of the calls I have received from God?

God's call does not guarantee absolute clarity. When one is called by God to do something, that "something" may not be clear or obvious. When God asked Mary to be the mother of the Messiah, for example, God did not present her with a spiral-bound notebook entitled "How to Be the Mother of God." In fact, God gave her no plan at all, no specific directions. God did not even tell her what to say to Joseph! But God offered Mary something far better than a plan for the future. God offered her a relationship for life! God's passionate intimacy with Mary in the present would lead her safely into an unknown and difficult future. The same is true for us. Our vocation as Christians is both a gift and a lifetime pursuit. Aware of our human limitations, we place all our trust in the faithfulness of God who calls us to greater courage, a broader vision, deeper insights, and stronger love. To such a call, only a passionate heart need apply.

CHAPTER 9

Eleven Truths about Love

In a few days we will celebrate St. Valentine's Day, one of my favorite days of the year. Although this day is highly commercialized in our country, I still see it as a day to celebrate the gift of love. It is a time to remember and thank all those individuals who nourish us with their friendship and love. And since love is what our Christian faith is all about, I will share with you eleven truths about love gleaned from my own lived experience. In turn, I invite you to reflect on these statements and then, based on your own experience, add to them or modify them.

- *Love begins and ends with God.* Saint John said it best: "We love because God first loved us." All love flows from God's love. Loving is not so much something I do as something I participate in. More accurately, love is not a thing at all. Love is a person. Again I quote the letter of John: "God is love." If we have difficulty loving, then perhaps we have lost sight of the person of God and God's unconditional love for us. Or maybe we have turned loving into a project.

- *Loving is the hardest thing we do.* Why did Jesus say, "Love one another….Love one another….Love one another" so many times? Because he knew how hard it was. Loving is so challenging that none of us gets it right every time. This realization helps us be more patient with clumsy and faltering attempts at loving—both our own and those of others.

- *Love is a mystery that takes many forms.* Love, like a restless toddler, will wriggle out of all our attempts to hold it and define it. Love refuses to be limited to one form. The most we can hope for is to be open to all the ways of loving that God might be showing us and asking of us.

- *Good loving is a lot like good dancing.* In her book *Gift from the Sea*, Anne Morrow Lindbergh says that a good relationship "has a pattern like a dance." The two partners "do not need to hold tightly." In fact, to clutch one's partner possessively "would be to arrest the pattern and freeze the movement." We might ask ourselves: Is my love for others too possessive? Do I ever use love to control others?

- *Love is a lot like hope.* Thomas Merton said that love is based on belief in the reversibility of evil. Every time we love, we prove we have not given up on human beings, no matter how unlovable they may seem to be. When we love we give expression to our undying hope for a better world, which includes a better family, a better church, a better country, and even a better me!

- *Love entails losing control.* In English, we say that people fall in love. We don't say they walk in love or march in love or stroll in love. No, people fall in love. Kerplunk! The word fall reminds us that loving entails a certain loss of control, a certain letting go, a certain foolishness. If we are the kind of person for whom losing control or letting go is unthinkable, we risk never falling in love. We might ask ourselves: What foolish things have I done because of love?

- *Love wins.* A priest was asked to summarize the Bible in one sentence. He did it in two words: "Life wins." I like that. Only I would prefer to say, "Love wins." If we do not believe that ultimately love wins, then how will we ever persevere in loving when loving is painful, or when evil and violence seem to have the upper hand? Do I really believe love wins?

- *Love involves self-sacrifice.* We do not like to hear the word self-sacrifice. It seems old-fashioned, negative, out of line with pop psychology. Yet, it is precisely through the sacrifice of self, that life grows and happiness abounds. Jesus' words, "Unless the grain of wheat fall to the ground and die" are just as true today as when he first uttered them. Do I still believe him?

- *We love not only as individuals, we love as a corporate body as well.* What I have said about love applies not only to us as individuals but also to us as a community whether that is a family, a parish, a religious congregation, or the Church itself. What sacrifices are we currently making as a family, parish, congregation, or church? What further sacrifices might God be asking of us?

- *Love must permeate everything we do.* The theologian Richard McBrien says that love must be at the heart of every Christian virtue. Justice without love is legalism; hope without love is self-abasement; care without love is mere duty; fidelity without love is servitude. He concludes, "No virtue is really a virtue unless it is permeated by love."

- *Love is measured by how much I love the least of my sisters and brothers.* In his parable of the Last Judgment, Jesus says, "Just as you did it to one of the least of these who are members of my family, you did it to me" (Mt 25:40). These words are sobering. True love is measured not by how much we love lovable people, that is, attractive, intelligent, healthy, clean, and good individuals, but rather, by how much we love those we see as the least. Someone once said, "Think of the person you love the least. That's how much you love God."

When the great Czech leader Vaclav Havel was imprisoned by the communists, he wrote letters to his wife, Olga. What impressed me was how he signed many of those letters: "Your faithful, lifelong fellow traveler." God's love invites us to love as God has loved us—deeply, consistently, lavishly. God's love binds us together as fellow travelers. May this feast of St. Valentine renew our love and commitment to God, to one another, and to God's people wherever we may be.

- ❦ *Which truth about love speaks to me today? Are there any other truths that I could add?*

CHAPTER 10

Seven Deadly "Isms"

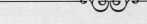

A while ago I read an article by Patrick McCormick entitled, "Bless me, Father, for I have ism-ed" (*U.S. Catholic*, March 2001). In this article, McCormick proposes a different sort of examination of conscience for Lent, one that addresses not personal sins and failings but "social sins" and "sinful social structures." He says, "Paying attention to social sins reminds us that communities—and not just individuals—can sin, and that societies too need to repent and reform." McCormick then lists seven "deadly isms" of our contemporary American society: individualism, consumerism, racism, sexism, classism, militarism, and voyeurism. He briefly describes each "ism" and then offers some reflective questions.

To help us grow in social awareness let's look at seven "isms" of our time and culture. Five of these "isms" are ones McCormick suggests; two are my own. I invite all of us to reflect on these "isms," not so much as individuals, but as a community, that is, a family, parish, school, congregation, or any other group to which we belong. To facilitate this reflection, I will say a few words about each "ism" and then offer some questions for our consideration.

Individualism. Individualism is the disposition to withdraw into oneself while letting the rest of society fend for itself. Recent authors have traced the growing tendency toward individualism in our society, for example, Robert Putnam in his book *Bowling Alone*. Putnam states that this individualism is reflected in the simple truth that many Americans barely know their neighbors. Other authors say that our individualism is evidenced by the fact that our country is the only modern democracy without an adequate welfare system or national health care program. In addition, we in the United States give less per capita in foreign aid to poor countries than most of our European counterparts.

Questions for reflection: How do I as an individual invest in the life of the communities to which I belong: my family, parish, religious congregation, local civic community? How do my communities contribute to the larger community such as the diocese, city, state, country, world? As Father Leonard Boff has said, "If we want to serve the true God, we must break out of the circle of self-absorption and pay heed to the bloodied faces of our fellow human beings. If we do not share life with the oppressed, we do not share life with God." How can we better share life with the oppressed?

Consumerism. One day as I was filling my car with gas, I found myself asking, "What right have I to use this precious gasoline? What entitles me to consume eight gallons of this non-renewable natural resource?" I found myself wondering if, by consuming this gas, I was somehow indirectly contributing to the mass poverty I experienced in India. Or by consuming this gas today, was I depriving my great-great-grandniece of this precious resource in the future?

The truth is that since 1950, Americans have used more of the earth's resources than everyone who lived before that date. Though we make up less than five percent of the world's population, we consume sixty percent of the planet's natural gas, forty percent of its coal, and thirty percent of its petroleum.

Questions for reflection: How strong is our sense of kinship with all of God's creation? What steps can we take as families and communities to reduce our consumption of natural resources such as electricity, natural gas, and gasoline? Do we recycle? If we have surplus goods, such as clothing, do we give these items to those who need them? How do we as a family, parish, or religious community live simply amid the affluence of our culture? Have we ever intentionally "fasted" from consuming resources such as electricity or gas for even one day?

Racism. Racism is an ugly thing. It can also be a hidden thing—hidden even from the person who is racist. Furthermore, we can be racist toward anyone: African Americans, Native Americans, Asians, Hispanics, Jews, or Muslims, to name a few.

Questions for reflection: Have we as a parish community ever asked forgiveness for our racist attitudes or actions? How might we do this? How strong are our corporate commitments to people who suffer from the effects of racism? Is there more we could be doing in this area?

Sexism. Sexism is discrimination based on gender. Historically, women especially have endured discrimination simply because they were women. Although great strides have been made in the past thirty years, the fact remains that many women continue to experience discrimination in the workplace and in the home. Women, for example, are traditionally paid less than men who have an equal or inferior education. Women also suffer from ninety-five percent of all domestic violence. However, sexism can also be directed against men. We sometimes call this form of sexism "male bashing."

Questions for reflection: Do we women ever discriminate against our own gender by thinking or saying things like, "I'm only a woman" or by automatically assuming that men are better than women? Do we ever engage in male bashing? What are we as a community doing to improve women's place in the home, work place, church?

Militarism. The United States spends twenty-two billion dollars a year on nuclear weapons. People in our country own more than 200 million handguns and commit 22,000 homicides a year. In addition, the United States has the world's highest number of persons serving jail time, with over two million Americans behind bars.

Questions for reflection: What weapons have I stockpiled to use against others: sarcasm, cutting remarks, giving the silent treatment? Have I personally ever committed a "homicide" by mocking someone, repeating vicious rumors, or by speaking in a demeaning way? Have I ever "imprisoned" others by refusing to forgive them or failing to give them another chance? Have we as a parish or religious congregation ever taken a corporate stance against violence in our society?

Speed-ism. Many modern TV programs are known for their fast-paced dialogue. Most characters speak rapidly with one other while racing down the hall or street. These shows remind me that we live in a fast-paced society where speed and efficiency are virtually deified. What a stark contrast to the gospels which depict Jesus as a man who slowed down to notice the lilies of the field, who listened to and told stories, who routinely shared meals with friends, who took time to play with little children, and who regularly communed with God in prayer.

Questions for reflection: At what pace am I living my life? How fast do I walk, talk, eat, and drive? As a family, parish, or religious congregation do we ever worship the gods of speed and efficiency? How can we help one another live a more gentle life?

Ugly-ism. James Hillman writes that, as human beings, we naturally crave beauty, and in its absence we suffer what he calls "beauty neurosis." In a similar vein, the psychologist Carl Jung once suggested to a colleague, "Why not go out into the forest for a time, literally? Sometimes a tree tells you more than you can read in books." God is the author of beauty: color, texture, tone, taste, aroma. Everyone needs a dose of beauty in order to experience the Transcendent breaking into our lives at every turn.

Questions for reflection: Do I make time for beauty in my life by visiting the art museum, attending a symphony or play, preparing a special meal, reading a good story, writing a little poem, or strolling in a park? Do we as a family, parish, or community ever choose beauty over functionality? How do we support the arts? How do we encourage one another to enjoy the beauty that surrounds us?

In his article in *U.S. Catholic,* Patrick McCormick says, "Since the sins of our communities are also often found in our disordered appetites, conversion doesn't so much mean eliminating these passions as learning to place them at the service of our love of God and neighbor." My prayer for us this Lent is threefold. May we recognize and acknowledge our disordered appetites both as individuals and as communities. May we take some definite steps to place our passions and resources more and more at the service of God and others. And in so doing, may we come to realize even more that, in the words of Wendy Wright, "we are embedded in a wider and more sustaining matrix of love than we can possibly imagine."

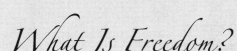

CHAPTER 11

What Is Freedom?

God is free.
And we who are made in God's image and likeness
    are invited to share in God's freedom.
In fact, the more free we become, the more like God we are.

What is freedom?
I like this definition:
    "Freedom is nothing else than the chance to be better."
Why have we been gifted with freedom?
Only this: to love.
We might think, "I want to be free to do what I want to do."
    Yes, but we are truly free only if what we want to do is love.
We might say, "I want to be free to be myself."
    Yes, but only if that self is a lover.
Or we might say, "I want to be free to be whole."
    Yes, but only if our wholeness leads to loving.

None of us is completely free.
Blessed are those who recognize their servitude,
    whether it be fear, compulsion, laziness,
      self-centeredness, pettiness, hardness of heart.
Servitude comes in many forms.

As St. John of the Cross reminds us,
   a bird tethered by a gossamer thread
   is just as unable to fly
   as one held by a steel cable.

Freedom is not very neat.
It can get messy at times.
Tyranny is always better organized.
Freedom is never achieved once and for all either.
From conception to death, we are all engaged
      in a lifelong process of liberation.

Someone has said, "Freedom is what you do
      with what's been done to you."
This means, among other things, that being freed
      somehow helps us to free others.
Says another, "Freedom is just another word for nothing left to lose."
Those individuals are most free who tread this earth lightly
      and with open hands.

Freedom is collective, communal.
A threat to freedom anywhere
   is a threat to freedom everywhere.
Conversely, the more free I become,
   the greater the potential for freedom for all of us.

Freedom costs.
One cost is "eternal vigilance."
Another is perseverance,
   perseverance in the daily wrestling with light and darkness
   that leads to the coming of the reign of God.

Jesus was free. Utterly so.

He was free to come, free to go.

    Free to speak, free to remain silent.

    Free to give, free to receive.

    Free to teach, free to listen.

    Free to be gentle, free to be firm.

    Free to be angry, free to be surprised.

    Free to laugh, free to cry.

Jesus was never more free than when he was nailed to the cross

    on Good Friday

      —except perhaps, than when he was raised in glory

        on Easter morning.

❧ *This Easter God invites me to greater freedom. How will I accept that invitation this day, this month, this year?*

❧ *What does freedom mean to me?*

CHAPTER 12

Jesus, the Master of Metaphor

I am an old English teacher or, as I prefer to say, a former English teacher. As such, I would like to ask you something you probably learned in high school English 101: What is a metaphor? In case you don't remember, I'll tell you. A metaphor is an implied comparison. A metaphor takes two different entities and shows how they are similar, connected, one.

We use metaphors all the time. We say things like, "She's such an angel!" When we say that, we don't mean she's a real angel. No, she's a human being, but we believe she has certain angelic qualities like goodness, sweetness, or generosity. Other metaphors are these: The stock market took a nose dive today. He threw me a curveball. I have too much on my plate right now. I finally see the light at the end of the tunnel.

Scripture is filled with metaphors. In fact, Jesus himself can be called a master of metaphor. He said things like this: "I am the vine, you are the branches. The kingdom of God is like a wedding feast. Fear not, little flock." Some of Jesus' metaphors are called extended metaphors. One day someone asked him, "Who is my neighbor?" Instead of answering that question directly, Jesus told a story. "A man was going down from Jerusalem to Jericho, and fell into the hands of robbers, who stripped him, beat him, and went away, leaving him half-dead" (Lk 10:30–37).

Good metaphors play a very important role in life. They enable us to see connections. They make complex ideas easier to comprehend. They help us to remember things better and longer.

Let's look at today's readings through the lens of metaphor. In the gospel, a man says to Jesus, "Teacher, what must I do to inherit eternal life?" Notice, Jesus doesn't give an answer to the "student." Instead, like a good teacher, he asks another question. "What is written in the law? What do you read there?" Jesus asks the man to look inside himself, to examine his own knowledge gleaned from his personal experience with Scripture. And the man gives this answer: "You shall love the Lord your God with all your heart, and with all your soul, and with all your strength, and with all your mind; and your neighbor as yourself" (Lk 10:25–27). And Jesus says to the man: "Wow! That's an A+ answer! Do it and you will pass with flying colors the course called life!" (That's a free translation!)

So today's gospel says: Love God. Love neighbor. Two seemingly distinct realities. Yet Jesus teaches that they are similar, connected, one. We might ask ourselves, Who is my neighbor? Is it only the person next to me, the person who is a lot like me? Or have I broadened my understanding of neighbor to include individuals who are different from me in age, looks, dress, customs, thinking, or gender?

In the second reading, Saint Paul says this: "Jesus is the image of the invisible God....In him all things hold together. He is the head of the body, the church" (Col 1:15–18). Talk about metaphors! Saint Paul is saying that if we want to know what God is like, just look at Jesus. For Jesus is much more than a metaphor for God, Jesus is the very image of God. Jesus is God.

In the first reading, the prophet Habakkuk says some beautiful things: "Write the vision....There is still a vision for the appointed time....If it seems to tarry, wait for it; it will surely come" (Hab 2:2–3). What exactly is the vision of which Habakkuk speaks? I'd like to suggest that the vision is not necessarily some type of apparition or dream. For the most important thing in life is not what we see; it's how we see it. It's how we look at things. One of my favorite Irish proverbs is this: "The church is near, but the road is icy. The tavern is far, but I'll walk very carefully." How we see determines what we see. We might ask ourselves:

What is my vision like? Do I see only the obvious or am I attentive to the subtle? Do I settle only for the immediate, or do I wait patiently for the deeper meanings to emerge? Do I perceive only the separateness of entities, or do I perceive the underlying connectedness of all things? To what extent do I share the vision of Jesus?

Recently we celebrated the jubilees of twenty-one sisters. We came together as family, friends, colleagues, and their sisters in religion. What did we really celebrate? We celebrated the vision of those women, a vision that enabled them to see beyond the immediate self-gratification that our society holds out to us as the meaning of life and the key to happiness. We celebrated the fact that these women chose to align their vision with the vision of Jesus who says that the meaning of life and the key to happiness lies in selfless loving.

I began by talking about metaphors. I'd like to conclude with a metaphor I really like: "God is spreading grace around the world like a five year old spreads peanut butter: thickly, sloppily, eagerly." Yes, God is spreading grace everywhere—even in my heart.

❦ *What are some of my favorite metaphors that Jesus used? Why?*

CHAPTER 13

The Common Good, Commitment, and Charism

One year I gave each of my sisters a photograph of Earth taken by the Apollo 17 mission. As I gaze at this picture of Earth, I find myself saying: Behold the earth! Our earth, the third planet from the sun, our sun.

In the book *A Man on the Moon*, Andrew Chaikin writes: "Whatever names humans gave their earth, it deserved to be called the Blue Planet, for its dominant aspect was the vivid, deep blue of oceans. In striking contrast were the clouds, brilliant white flecks and streamers that embraced the globe, swirling along coastlines and across oceans. Where land masses peeked through, the vivid oranges and tans of the deserts were easy to spot. More elusive were the jungles and temperate zones; because their verdant hues did not easily penetrate the atmosphere, they showed up a bluish gray with only a hint of green. And everywhere, beyond the planet's bright, curved edge, a blackness so deep as to be unimaginable."

Later on in the book, one of the astronauts said the earth looked like "a gemstone suspended in dark water." The sight of it "held him in awe as he watched it turn on an invisible axis. His overwhelming feeling was a sense of purpose, a gut-level awareness that (earth) was simply too beautiful to have happened by accident. He felt as if he were seeing earth as it had appeared in the moment before the Creation, in the mind's eye of God." Behold earth! Our earth, the third planet from the sun, our sun.

I would like to share with you a few features of this striking photograph of Earth. First, in the lower part of the picture you see the polar ice cap. The sight of this ice cap should remind us of an alarming reality: the depletion of the protective ozone layer, a fact that has apocalyptic ramifications for the future of our planet. Moving up on the picture, you can detect the outline of the continent of Africa. By design, I selected a picture of Earth that does not feature North America. Why? To remind us that North America (more specifically, the United States) is not the center of the world. A whole world exists beyond our borders with people of different languages, customs, needs, and with unique contributions to make to the history of humanity.

The sight of the Arabian peninsula reminds us of the so-called developed nations' uncontrolled appetite for oil. The Middle East recalls the sad fact that, for some peoples of the earth, war and violence are a way of life. A tiny spot is the Holy Land, that sacred place where the Second Person of the Blessed Trinity broke into our world, pitching his tent among us over 2000 years ago. And Planet Earth has never been the same!

Common Good

The picture of Earth reminds me of three things I would like to explore: the common good, commitment, and charism. First, let's look at the common good. Some people might be uncomfortable with the phrase "common good." They remember that, in the past, sometimes grave injustices were done to individuals in the name of the common good. I am in no way minimizing such injustices. But I am urging us to move beyond our society's glorification of individualism that borders on the pathological, an individualism that has no regard for the common good. I am ashamed, for example, when I hear a White House spokesperson say that our high energy consumption is a way of life that should be protected at all costs. "The American way of life is a blessed one," he said. But we as Christians know that the money in our pocket, the electricity we consume, the food we eat is not ours alone. All of it also belongs to others—to the single mother on Cleveland's near west side, the little boy on the Pine Ridge Reservation in South Dakota, the rickshaw driver in the streets of Calcutta, the infant with the distended stomach in Sudan. All, all that we call "ours" belongs to everyone.

As Christians we must ask ourselves some hard questions. To what extent do we as individuals, families, parishes, and religious congregations incarnate the values of the gospel in our consumer society? Or, sadly, to what extent have we bought into the values of "the American way of life" through our purchasing habits, our driving habits, the allocation of our time? In her article, "Leadership for the Common Good," Sister Donna Markham raises some thought-provoking questions. She says that with our current overemphasis on individualism:

- Are we perhaps depriving ourselves of the possibility of corporate magnanimous accomplishment?

- Have individual good works superseded the ability to do something passionately together?

Pope John Paul II underscores the ecological link as a driving force for mission for the common good in his address entitled, "Peace with All Creation." He writes: "The earth is ultimately a common heritage, the fruits of which are for the benefit of all….It is manifestly unjust that a privileged few should continue to accumulate excess goods, squandering available resources, while masses of people are living in conditions of misery at the very lowest level of subsistence. Today, the dramatic threat of ecological breakdown is teaching us the extent to which greed and selfishness—both individual and corporate—are contrary to the order of creation, an order which is characterized by mutual interdependence….Simplicity, moderation and discipline, as well as a spirit of sacrifice must become part of everyday life."

There's a popular bumper sticker that says, "Honk if you love Jesus." But there's a better one that says, "Tithe if you love Jesus. Any fool can honk." Our ministry to the poor, the abandoned, and the uneducated will make demands upon us as individuals and communities. What sacrifices are we willing to make so that others may have life?

Commitment

Every night before I retire I go to the baptismal font in our chapel and bless myself with its waters as a concrete reminder to me of why I am doing what I am doing. For me, that baptismal font has become a personal symbol of the vowed commitment I made many years ago.

Recently I attended the wedding of one of my nieces, Melissa. As she pronounced her marriage vows to John, her voice broke a few times, especially when she came to those familiar words, "For better or for worse, for richer or for poorer, in sickness and in health, till death do us part." Witnessing the vows of Melissa and John caused me to reflect on the vows I made when I became a Sister of Notre Dame. I began to wonder if the vow formula is too "sanitized," too "romanticized," too "nice"? Maybe my religious vows should be more like the traditional marriage vows, that is, more concrete, more realistic reflecting the situations I face daily.

The other day I received a notice for a job opening at a nearby Catholic high school. The opening was for a head wrestling coach. I pondered that request for several minutes and thought, "Maybe I should apply for this position. After all, I have had some experience with wrestling!" Haven't we all? Isn't wrestling part and parcel of our commitment as Christians? With whom do we wrestle? We wrestle with each other, don't we? How? We disagree with each other, we annoy each other, we challenge each other. In fact, the more honest and open we are with each other and the more we trust each other, the more comfortable we will be with an occasional tussle!

We also wrestle with the issues of our day and age, issues concerning education, community, church, social justice, ecology, life, and death. If we're really honest, we will admit that we wrestle at times even with God. Yes, as someone has said, God is not always a dancing partner. Sometimes God is our wrestling partner. But don't worry, because God can take it. In fact, God probably looks forward to wrestling with us because sometimes that's the only way we can move beyond where we are, the only way we can achieve transformation into Jesus.

Charism

Vatican II called religious communities to return to the charism of their founders. The Council also provided a definition of the word. A charism is "a supernatural gift bestowed by the Holy Spirit for the building up of the Body of Christ." In other words, it is a specific grace given to an individual to promote the common good. For many years, the Sisters of Notre Dame looked solely to Saint Julie Billiart whose charism we share with the Sisters of Notre Dame de Namur. But more recently we have been asked to broaden and deepen our understanding of our charism by looking more closely at the unique contribution to the Coesfeld branch of the Sisters of Notre Dame made by Aldegonda Wolbring and Lisette Kuhling. And we are doing that.

There is one caution, however. Vatican II's directive to look back at the founding charism can be misleading. The truth is that the charism of a congregation is found not only in the past, that is, in the founders of religious congregations. The charism is also found in the present, in the members who are living today. In her article, "Charism or Deep Story?" Margaret Thompson says that a congregation's identity is rooted in a "narrative structure" or "deep story." Though rooted in that deep story, a congregation is not merely a "community of memory." Rather, a congregation must always be on its way "to the realization of a new charismatically gifted reality in which all members must participate and assume responsibility." In her recent address, Sister Mary Sujita, our Superior General, said, "Having a charism and living it is far more important than describing it."

In her book *The Fire in These Ashes*, Sister Joan Chittister says that the essential purpose of religious life is "to seek God," to seek God everywhere—in pain and joy, in confusion and certainty, in success and failure. Everywhere. May each of us continue the "God quest." May we let nothing—not even ministry—get in the way of this quest. And may we support and encourage one another in this sacred seeking.

❧ *Is there anything in this chapter I really agree with or disagree with? What and why?*

CHAPTER 14

Thanksgiving and the Paschal Mystery

Since September 11, 2001, our lives have changed. Fear abounds. New security measures have been enacted everywhere. Reports about the fighting in Iraq and other places fill the airwaves. And poignant pictures of the maimed victims of suicide bombings dominate the evening news. Added to these horrors are our own haunting memories of the airplanes crashing into the Twin Towers, the buildings burning and collapsing, the hundreds of people killed, and the mountain of rubble and ash that took over a year to clean up.

Considering what we have experienced as a nation since September 11, we might be asking ourselves, how can we celebrate the national holiday we call Thanksgiving amid such gloom? How can we sing "Over the river and through the woods" when we are afraid to board an airplane or open our mail? How can we sit down and enjoy a turkey dinner when so many of our brothers and sisters are grieving, fleeing from bombs, and even dying?

I am not going to provide facile answers to these questions. Instead, I would simply like to share with you a few thoughts gleaned from my own reading these past few weeks and my personal prayer. I do this as a way to support your own continued reflection on these momentous world events, as well as to encourage you to share with one another your thoughts about what these events are calling us to do as Christians.

On Tuesday, September 11, 2001 I began my workday with considerable enthusiasm. I had no meetings or appointments scheduled that particular morning, so I was looking forward to finishing some important paperwork. When I heard what was happening in New York City and Washington D.C., however, I ran to the nearest TV and, like many of you, watched in disbelief and horror as the events unfolded. For the rest of the day, I walked around stunned, unable to focus on anything. Against the backdrop of the terrorist attacks, nothing seemed important anymore. Nothing seemed worth doing anymore.

The events of September 11 forced all of us to re-evaluate everything. The tragedy underscored those things that really matter: the sanctity and fragility of human life, the gift of family and friendship, the true heroism involved in laying down one's life for others. Perhaps this Thanksgiving we might ask ourselves these questions: What is really important to me? To what or to whom do I devote my time and energy? What are we focusing on as individuals, as families, as communities, and as a church? Are these things worthy of the time and attention we give them?

One common response to the terrorist attacks was to ask, "Where is God in all of this?" Father James Martin, SJ, associate editor of *America*, described his visit to Ground Zero a few days after the attack to celebrate Mass for the rescue workers. At one point he and another Jesuit from Poland set up a small table amid the damaged buildings to use as a makeshift altar. As Father was setting up the table, his friend pointed to a nearby plywood board with large neon orange letters that said, "Morgue." Father suddenly realized he had unknowingly picked a site for Mass right next to the temporary morgue. Then he spotted another sign placed nearby. It read "Body of Christ." Father didn't know who had put that particular sign there, but he sensed it was very appropriate and theologically sound. Yes, Christ was very present there—in the rescue workers who were risking their own lives for others and in the maimed bodies lying in that temporary morgue.

September 11 reminded all of us what the paschal mystery is really about. Sometimes we Christians too easily say, "We are an Easter people." That is true, of course. Belief in Jesus' Resurrection and our own resurrection is central to our faith. But the paschal mystery is not just about the Resurrection. It includes the suffering and death of Jesus as well. In the Creed we affirm that Jesus suffered, died and was buried. Then he rose again and ascended into heaven. That's the paschal mystery. As Robert Waznak, professor emeritus at Washington Theological Union, said, to bypass the suffering and burial is not authentic Christianity. We cannot "fast forward" to Easter Sunday without pausing at Good Friday.

Just as we cannot gloss over suffering and pain in the world at large, so too, we cannot gloss over the suffering and pain in our own lives. An old Carly Simon song says, "I haven't got time for the pain." Our belief in the paschal mystery suggests just the opposite. It urges us, "Make time for your pain. Name it, trace its source, work with it, knowing that God is truly present in all your struggles. Continue to believe that embracing your pain can, with God's help, eventually lead to glory and resurrection."

❧ *What are the struggles in my personal life, family, local community, and the wider church? Are we facing these struggles, or do we tend to ignore or avoid them? Are we able to sit with others in their pain, or are we too quick to give shallow answers and superficial remedies?*

The current world situation challenges us to face our own complicity with evil. We can dismiss these terrorist attacks as the work of a small group of fanatics. "Kill them and end terrorism!" some are saying. The events of September 11 challenge us to ask ourselves some tough questions. For example, were the seeds of today's terrorism sown a thousand years ago when, in the name of Christ, the Christian crusaders invaded and laid waste so many Muslim lands? What current national policies continue to incite hatred toward the United States? Sociologists tell us that poverty is a breeding ground for terrorism. What are we doing to ease the abject poverty endured by the vast majority of people who share our planet? Pope John Paul II reminded us that 800 million people in the world suffer from malnutrition, and 200 million of them are children. What are we doing to alleviate that grave injustice? This Thanksgiving is a good time to examine our own "personal policies" as well. Do I ever engage in the more subtle kind of terrorist acts such as slamming doors or refusing to speak to someone? Have I ever been a "verbal sniper"?

In the days immediately following the attacks of September 11, most of the American people responded in one of two ways. On the one hand, we donated millions of dollars for the families of the victims. On the other hand, many Americans called for revenge. In the newsletter from the Center for Concern, Father Jim Hug, SJ, addresses both of these faces of America. He wrote: "It is possible to refuse to respond to terrorism with terrorism. It is imperative that we not respond to an unspeakable crime against innocent people with another unspeakable crime against innocent people." He reminds us that Jesus gave us a strategy for responding to violence: love and forgiveness. This is the only response that can end the vicious cycle of violence. Father Hug writes, "We can end terrorism if we turn the courage, heroism, generosity, compassion and love that are the best face of America toward those buried in the tragedies of poverty and degradation everywhere on the planet and reach out to them."

As our nation pauses together to celebrate Thanksgiving, let us thank God for the blessings we have received, blessings that, before September 11, we may have taken for granted: life, liberty, family, friends, community, and material and spiritual gifts of all kinds. On Thanksgiving, let us commit ourselves once again to the gospel priorities of love, justice, and forgiveness. Let us remember that we alone do not have the power to end evil, suffering and death. But, in the words of Father Waznak, "we do have the grace that comes from the paschal mystery which invites us to pick up the shattered pieces of our world and make something holy out of them."

We can begin this sacred task of rebuilding our world by reverencing every person God places on our path each day. The traditional greeting in India is *namaste*. It is a short word with a deep meaning. Namaste means:

I honor the place in you where the whole universe resides.

I honor the place in you of love, of light, of truth, and of peace.

I honor the place in you where, if you are in that place in you, and I am in that place in me, there is only one of us.

Namaste. And Happy Thanksgiving!

CHAPTER 15

Saint Joseph

During this season of Advent, I would like to say a few words about Saint Joseph. Some might be wondering, what does this first century Palestinian Jew have to say to us who are twenty-first century American Christians? Although Joseph could say many things to us, I have chosen three.

It's okay to take a back seat. John's gospel doesn't mention Joseph. Mark's gospel mentions him only obliquely, referring to Jesus as the "carpenter's son." In Luke's gospel, the focus is on Mary with Joseph decidedly taking a back seat. Only in Matthew's gospel is Joseph given any real attention. And this attention underscores the fact that Joseph was a fairly ordinary human being. In fact, we can say that he was an ordinary man living in an ordinary village during ordinary times. Joseph's ordinariness is reflected in many traditional paintings of the first Christmas where he is often pictured off to the side or in the background. Joseph did not need to be center stage. Rather he was content to play a supporting role in the great drama of salvation. Being where God wanted him to be was more important to him than being where he wanted to be. Being faithful was more important than being popular or powerful.

Sometimes in life we are center stage. This is not bad, of course. But sooner or later we may be asked to step out of the limelight and into the wings. Perhaps a change in ministry, an illness, or the natural aging process may cause us to let go of a previously "starring" role. How do we handle such a change? Are we satisfied to play a supporting role or do we insist on being center stage? How strong is our need to be needed?

57

Joseph allowed God to shatter his world. The Annunciation turned Mary's life upside down. It also turned Joseph's life upside down. Mary's pregnancy initially caused Joseph unspeakable anguish, an anguish that was assuaged only by the visit of an angel during the night. Even after the angel left him, Joseph still had to believe that Mary's child was no ordinary child but the "Son of the Most High." Joseph was never given a manual on "How to Raise a Messiah." No, Joseph had to learn "on the job" through patient trial and error. Like us, he had to learn how to live by living. He had to learn to trust God even when circumstances were unsettling or unclear.

Theologian Karl Rahner, SJ, has said: "If God's incomprehensibility does not…call us out of the little house of our homely, close-hugged truths…we have misunderstood the words of Christianity." Time and again Joseph was called out of the small world of his own making and into the wider world of God's ultimate incomprehensibility. Joseph had to let go of his preconceived ideas in order to embrace the expansiveness of a God whose ways are always beyond our imagining. During Advent we might want to reflect on a time when our world was shattered. What was that shattering experience like for us? What did God call us to do in that situation?

Joseph lived with fears and tensions. The gospels make it clear that Joseph did not live a carefree life. On the contrary, his life was filled with grave fears and unrelenting tension. The trip to Bethlehem was no pleasant excursion into the countryside; rather it was an arduous trek across inhospitable lands with a wife who was nine months pregnant. The flight into Egypt had to be traumatic. We catch a glimpse of what this upheaval must have been for Joseph when we see the terror stricken faces of today's refugees in our newspapers and on television. Even a happy occasion when he and Mary found their son Jesus in the Temple was preceded by three days and nights of unspeakable agony for Joseph. Added to these fears and tension were the daily trials of a man trying to scratch out a living for his wife and son in a country subjected to the cruel domination of a foreign military power.

The gospels lead us to believe that Joseph bore the tension with considerable grace. Through all the ups and downs of his life, he clung to what really mattered: his belief in a God who was both powerful and good. Joseph's hope lay not in developing his own intellectual prowess, not in having the best religious and political leaders, not in finding the perfect community. No, his hope lay in the mercy and fidelity of God. How gracefully am I bearing the fears and tension of my own life? What might help me to bear them more gracefully? In what or in whom does my hope lie?

Michael Card has written a beautiful song entitled, "Joseph's Song"; many of us are familiar with it. The song captures both Joseph's apprehension and his awe at the birth of Jesus. "How can it be?" he muses over and over again. We too find ourselves asking the same question. "How can it be?" when we see our world reeling from war and terrorism. "How can it be?" when we encounter injustices within our church and our community. "How can it be?" when we experience again and again our own sinfulness despite our best efforts and resolve.

But we also ask in awe, "How can it be?" when we see strangers risking their lives to save strangers, when we witness the compassionate love within our church and our community, and when we experience again and again the grace to say "I'm sorry" and "I forgive." During Advent my prayer for all of us is that we may learn from Saint Joseph, this ordinary man, this befriender of fear and tension, who ultimately found his peace and fulfillment in the incomprehensibility of a totally loving God.

CHAPTER 16

Pain and the Call to Transformation

As a topic for the season of Lent, I would like to offer you a few thoughts on the subject of pain. Some might be thinking, "What a negative topic!" But I hope to show that pain, as difficult as it may be at times, plays an indispensable role in our transformation into Jesus.

Everyone experiences pain. None of us is exempt from it. None of us has a perfectly functioning body, a perfect family, perfect friends, a perfect parish, a perfect ministry. As we engage in the challenges of daily living, we encounter pain in a wide variety of forms. We experience physical pain from minor headaches to serious illness. We experience psychological pain such as depression, grief, or strains in relationships. We also feel other kinds of pain that are hard to categorize: the ache of loneliness, the fear of diminishment, the distress of failure, and the anguish of shame.

Remembering that everyone experiences pain can keep us from slipping into a "victim mode." Richard Rohr tells the story of one woman who came to him for help. By her own admission she was becoming a hateful and negative person. As they talked, she kept coming back to an injustice that she had suffered many years before. At one moment she blurted out, "My pain is my ticket." Rohr writes, "I realized that her pain had become her very identity. Playing the victim gave her a kind of power, a moral superiority over almost everybody." Playing the victim also excused the woman from having to do anything about her pain. Because she viewed herself as a victim, writes Rohr, "she didn't have to grow up, let go, surrender, forgive—all the things the great religions of the world deem necessary for spiritual growth."

If we are aware that everyone experiences some kind of pain, we will be gentler and more compassionate, won't we? How wonderful it would be if every time we met another person, for example, we would silently reverence her or his personal pain. Or if every time we encountered colleagues, clients, or complete strangers, we would honor their particular struggles toward greater wholeness. Acknowledging the universality of pain can help us be more patient with ourselves, too, because we know that spiritual growth seldom follows a straight line but is rather a journey of ups and downs, ins and outs, arounds and throughs.

> ❧ *What pain am I experiencing right now? Is it calling me "to grow up, let go, surrender, forgive"? Do I ever "play the victim"?*

There is no way around pain. But because pain hurts, we sometimes devise some creative ways to try to ease or avoid it. Sometimes, for example, we deny our pain. "Lonely? Who me? Of course not!" We can try to avoid pain in other ways, too: overeating, addiction to medication, uncontrollable spending, alcohol abuse, excessive TV watching, and withdrawal from others. But, over time, these avoidance techniques carry within themselves their own kind of pain. Sometimes the pain involved in trying to avoid pain is greater than the original pain we were trying to avoid!

In his book *Let Your Life Speak*, Parker Palmer talks about another source of pain, the pain of acknowledging the darkness within ourselves. He maintains that unless we courageously face our own sin and weaknesses, we run the risk of projecting these onto other individuals or even institutions. Palmer writes, "We must withdraw the negative projections we place on people and situations—projections that serve mainly to mask our fears about ourselves—and acknowledge and embrace our own liabilities and limits."

* *What are my means of avoiding pain? What are some of the ways I can acknowledge and embrace my own liabilities and limits?*

God uses our pain to lead us to greater wholeness. Kathleen Norris writes, "We human beings learn best how to love when we're a bit broken, when our plans fall apart, when our myths of self-sufficiency and safety are shattered." On September 11, 2001, we as a nation experienced our brokenness and vulnerability in a horrifying way. When the terrorists flew our own planes into the World Trade Center, the Pentagon, and the farmlands of western Pennsylvania, our myths of self-sufficiency and safety were shattered. What was our response as a nation to this act of terrorism? First, there was an outpouring of compassion for the victims. Then came the cries of revenge against the perpetrators. However, some voices among us questioned whether, through our intense hatred and wholesale bombings, we were turning into the very people we labeled as terrorists. At the same time the bombings began, our government leaders were encouraging us to go on living as we had before September 11. They also strongly urged us to continue to consume goods in order to keep our economy going. What an ironic response to our massive corporate pain. As one columnist put it, "Americans are being avidly encouraged not to change their ways, but to fight terrorism by buying more stuff." Wouldn't a better response to our pain be to question how we are living and to acknowledge the negative consequences of our unbridled consumerism? G.K. Chesterton reflects: "There are two ways to get enough. One is to continue to accumulate more and more. The other is to desire less."

Why does pain provide such an opportunity for transformation? For one thing, pain destabilizes the ego. It also heightens our awareness of how little control we have over life. Pain also challenges our certitudes. It makes it impossible for us to live according to facile formulas or pious platitudes.

❧ *How am I still responding to the events of September 11? What are some of the "facile formulas and pious platitudes" that pain has led me to question or discard?*

When it comes to pain, we Christians "have it made." For we believe in a God who became a human being like us and who knows and understands our pain firsthand. As Madeleine L'Engle has said, "Terrible things are not God's will, but God can enter them with redemptive love. That is the promise of the Incarnation."

John Shea reminds us that "Jesus lived without anesthesia. He was numb neither to the joy nor pain of the world. He never developed defenses to keep both happiness and sorrow moderate." Jesus experienced the pain that came from loneliness, misunderstanding, overwork, estrangement with some members of his family, rejection by religious leadership, and the betrayal of his closest friends. We reverence his most painful hours when we reverence his image on the crucifix. Richard Rohr has said that we Christians have a strange image of God. Our image of God is not a big golden sun or an amorphous, infinite power we call "the Force." No, our image of God "is a naked, bleeding, poor man dying on the cross." On Calvary, Jesus receives our hatred and does not return it. He absorbs our human sin rather than pass it on. He does not use his pain and death as power over others to punish them, but to transform them. When Jesus says, "Father, forgive them," he is showing us the way to true peace and happiness. How eager are we to follow his way?

❧ *Have I ever experienced God entering my pain with redemptive love? Have I ever used my pain to help others?*

Lent is traditionally a time to pray, fast, and give alms. During Lent and year round let us pray that our pain may lead us to a greater trust in the provident care of God. Let us fast from playing the victim and from projecting our sins and weaknesses onto others. And let us give alms by joyfully embracing the pain involved in consistent, unselfish loving, especially of the poor and marginalized. I would like to close with a tender poem that I feel encapsulates the theme of this reflection:

"The Price"

Anguish, yes,
    But not despair.

This agony that
    Ties your breath
    Is a law
    The fruitful
    Must bear.
Ask the
    Almost-mother,
    Her body heaving and torn—

Only from
    Exquisite pain
    Is beauty born.

CAROL L. PEARSON

CHAPTER 17

Our Christian Legacy of Joy and Laughter

Today we celebrate two feasts that are particularly significant for me as a Sister of Notre Dame: the feast of the Annunciation of Mary and the feast that marks the entrance of Saint Julie Billiart into eternal life. In honor of these two great women who have influenced the lives of many people, I would like to say a few words about joy and laughter.

Some might be thinking, "How can you write about joy and laughter when there is so much pain, suffering, and uncertainty in the world today?" By choosing this focus, I am certainly not denying the gravity of the current world situation: terrorism, war, famine, sexual abuse scandals in our church, corruption in business, and the ever-present threat of a nuclear bomb or accident. No, we cannot deny or hide from the very serious issues of our day. On the contrary, we can and must continue to work untiringly for just solutions to today's grave problems. But it is precisely because our world is in such desperate straits that we need to emphasize joy and laughter all the more. For, if we do not preserve the joy and laughter inherent in the good news, we risk becoming paralyzed or demoralized by all the bad news we encounter every day.

We begin this reflection by recalling that joy and laughter are hallmarks of our Christian faith. As someone has said, "A gloomy Christian should be a contradiction in terms." Recently I discovered a fascinating tradition in the Greek Orthodox Church. On the day after Easter, the faithful gather to trade jokes with one another. They do this on Easter Monday since they believe that the greatest "joke" of all took place on Easter Sunday, that is, Jesus' victory over death. In his book *The Joyful Jesus*, Cal Samra writes: "There is an old saying that 'he who laughs last, laughs best.' And who had the largest and most robust laugh in history? The resurrected Jesus." So, as Christians, our joy and laughter are ultimately rooted in the resurrection of Jesus.

Now let's look a little more closely at our Christian legacy of joy and laughter by asking a few questions: Exactly what is humor? Why do we laugh? We will answer these questions by looking at a few stories.

> A mother was preparing pancakes for her sons, Kevin, five, and Ryan, three. The boys began to argue over who would get the first pancake. Their mother saw the opportunity for a moral lesson. She said, "If Jesus were sitting here, he would say, 'Let my brother have the first pancake. I can wait.'" Kevin turned to his younger brother and said, "Ryan, you be Jesus."

Why do we smile at this story? We smile at the cleverness of little Kevin. Though only five, he creatively figures out a way to heed his mother's words while simultaneously getting the first pancake. How ingenious we humans can be! We smile at this story for another reason too: It gently pokes fun at our humanity. We humans have an innate tendency toward selfishness. It's hard for us to be selfless. Like Kevin, we sometimes use our ingenuity to get what we want. So, one reason we laugh at jokes or stories such as this one is because they remind us of the glory and frailty of the human condition.

Here's a story from the Buddhist tradition that shows another reason why we laugh.

> Student: How long will it take me to learn enlightenment?
> Master: Five years.
> Student: What if I try real hard?
> Master: Ten years.

Another reason we laugh is because we are surprised. We expect things to go one way, and they go another way. In the above story we, along with the student, expect the time for enlightenment to be shortened the harder the student works at it. We smile at the greater truth that too much effort at times can actually impede certain kinds of growth.

Another reason we laugh is because we see the bigger picture. The next story illustrates this.

> A little girl was visiting her great-grandmother in a nursing home. When she spotted the woman's dentures in a glass on the bedside table, her eyes got real big. "Boy!" she said to her great-grandmother, "You're gonna get lots of money from the tooth fairy!"

We smile because we see more than the little girl whose remark is based on her limited experience and perspective. When we enter heaven, we will begin to see things from God's perspective, the broadest perspective of them all. At that moment, I imagine we will laugh at many things we took very seriously while here on earth, because we will then see them as part of a much bigger picture. Have you ever experienced something that was traumatic when it occurred but which you could laugh about later? If so, what accounted for the change in your response?

If joy and laughter are so crucial to a healthy Christian spirituality, then how can we keep these qualities alive in our lives? There are many ways we can do this, but I would like to suggest four.

John Powell, SJ, once said, "If you're happy, let your face know." Maybe we can begin to be more joyful by taking a peek in the mirror and asking ourselves: Does my face look like the face of someone who believes in the good news of the gospel? Does my face show that I believe God is madly in love with me, that Jesus is my friend and Savior, and that love is stronger than death?

If we installed a meter in every family, parish, school, workplace, or religious community to measure the level of joy and laughter, where would the meter register: (1) high/healthy, (2) medium/ailing, (3) low/on life support, or (4) dead?

Secondly, we might ask ourselves: what is my image of God? Is God a stern taskmaster lurking in the dark, ready to pounce on me? Or is God like the father in the parable of the prodigal son, running toward me with open arms? The German philosopher Friedrich Nietzsche said, "I should only believe in a God who would know how to dance." Does our God know how to dance? Do we know how to dance, that is, do we trust in the goodness of life so much that we can afford to relax and enjoy ourselves on a regular basis?

Thirdly, we can grow in joy by being faithful to prayer. Good prayer keeps us in touch with the joys and sorrows of life. It holds before us both the glory and frailty of the human condition. G.K. Chesterton wrote that ultimately sorrow is an "innocent interlude" in life, but joy is "the permanent pulsation of the soul." Such a statement does not minimize our pain and sorrow. We as Christians have experienced God's goodness and provident care, so we are able to trust in that goodness and care even amid our tears.

The fourth way we can grow in sustaining joy and laughter is by periodically taking stock of our sense of humor. Scientists tell us that children laugh hundreds of times a day. The average adult laughs only fifteen times a day. As we get older, joy and laughter don't always come easily or readily. Levity, in fact, demands a certain amount of self-denial. Theologian Jean Leclercq calls this the "asceticism of joy." He explains that levity "involves the most difficult self-denial of all: You no longer take yourself so seriously. The days and nights no longer rotate around you, your headaches and hiatal hernia, your problems, your frustrations."

When we celebrate the feast of the Annunciation, let us ask Mary to increase our joy and laughter. After all, it was she who prayed those beautiful words of the Magnificat: "My soul magnifies the Lord, and my spirit rejoices in God my Savior, for he has looked with favor on the lowliness of his servant." (What a surprise!) "He has scattered the proud in the thoughts of their hearts....and lifted up the lowly." (What a topsy-turvy world!) "His mercy is for those who fear him from generation to generation." (Talk about the BIG picture!) Mary is the same woman we call "Cause of our Joy." Mary is the woman about whom Saint Julie said: "We must not rest satisfied with honoring Mary's prerogatives. We must also strive to imitate our heavenly Mother." Are we a "cause of joy" in community and in ministry?

Around the feast of the Annunciation we also honor Saint Julie Billiart. What better way to do this than to imitate her who was known as "the smiling saint"? I would like to conclude this reflection on joy and laughter with a few more amusing statements.

> Car mechanic to customer: "I couldn't repair your brakes, so I made your horn louder."

> A little boy was overheard praying: "God, if you can't make me a better boy, don't worry about it. I'm having a real good time like I am."

> Sign in a repair shop: "We do three types of jobs: Cheap, Quick and Good. You can have any two. A good quick job won't be cheap. A good job cheap won't be quick. A cheap job quick won't be good."

> A man and his wife argued so much that they saw a marriage counselor. The man said to a friend, "We still argue, but now we call it sharing."

My prayer for all of us consists in the words of Bishop Klaus Hemmerle of Aachen, Germany: "I wish each of us Easter eyes, able to perceive in death, life; in guilt, forgiveness; in separation, unity; in wounds, glory; in the human, God; in God, the human; and in the I, the you."

❧ *What helps me to hang on to my sense of humor?*

CHAPTER 18

What Is God's Name?

One year ago I handed out to my sisters a beautiful colored picture of Earth, our beloved Blue Planet, taken from Apollo 17. That was July 27—forty-six days before September 11, six months before stories of clerical sexual misconduct began to fill our newspapers and crowd our airwaves. What a difference forty-six days can make. What a difference six months can make! What a difference one year can make! For within that single year our very vocabulary was irrevocably altered. We had to learn all kinds of new words and phrases: Taliban, al-Qaeda, homeland security, dirty bomb. We already knew other words like sexual abuse, hush money, cover-up—but these words were no longer relegated to movies and television shows. They were the anguished vocabulary of our victimized sisters and brothers, they were words now being direct-ed at our priests, our bishops, our church, us.

All of us have been deeply affected by world events. None of us knows today what other devastating events may occur in the future. So we ask ourselves: What do today's national and global realities have to do with our commitment as Christians? My answer is simple: Everything!

But we have only a short time for reflection. So I'd like to offer you a few thoughts culled from my own experiences and from my own read-ings and conversations with others who are grappling with one of the most important questions we can ask: What is God's name? For we know that the name or names we give to God impacts everything we think, do, and are. I have organized my reflections around the words on a card I gave to each of my sisters. It said: Warmth is the summer name of God. Color is the autumn name of God. Silence is the winter name of God. Life is the spring name of God.

Warmth Is the Summer Name of God

I have a childhood friend named Mary Ann Ryan who lives a little north of Detroit. Mary Ann is my age, married, with two grown children. She and her husband own about ten acres and raise a small menagerie of animals: a couple dozen sheep (the ram's name is Lavender), a handful of chickens, two dogs, several cats, and one old goose named Dante who struts around the yard with his beak up in the air, as if he's in charge of everything. One spring day I was visiting Mary Ann when she said to me, "My cat had two kittens yesterday. Come out to the barn to see them." So we walked out to the barn together. The kittens were nestled in the straw behind a piece of plywood. When Mary Ann moved the plywood to show me the kittens, we were both startled by what we saw. A brown chicken was sitting on top of the two tiny kittens. She was keeping them warm.

It's easy to explain how this strange phenomenon may have happened. Apparently the mother cat had left the kittens for a few minutes. The kittens, both basically white, did resemble two eggs. The chicken must have happened by and saw the kittens lying in the straw. Instantly, something clicked in her little chicken brain. Thinking the warm kittens were eggs, she did what every hen is programmed to do: incubate! That hen sat on those "eggs," keeping them warm, sustaining the life inside with nothing more than the warmth of her own body.

This incident is a parable for me. No, we are not chickens. I am reminded, however, that even Jesus likened himself to a chicken: "Jerusalem, Jerusalem…how often have I desired to gather your children together as a hen gathers her brood" (Mt 23:37). So, like that chicken sitting on those kittens, we too have been programmed to incubate. Why? Because God incubates. Because Warmth is one of God's names. And we are made in the image and likeness of God. In fact, isn't the first image of God in Genesis that of God hovering over the "formless wasteland," the "vast abyss" like some cosmic bird? Or, in the beautiful words of the Jesuit poet Gerard Manley Hopkins: "Because the Holy Ghost over the bent/World broods with warm breast and with ah! bright wings."

This God named Warmth calls us to warm others. How do we do this? By sharing our knowledge, our expertise, our resources. By sharing the warmth of our inner selves: our spirituality, our prayer, our hopes, our hurts, our dreams, our fears, our joys—first and foremost with the women who share the same Christian commitment and vowed commitment with us. Community is an incredible thing. In her book *Selling All*, Sandra Schneiders, IHM, reminds us of this fact when she writes: "History testifies that, paradoxically and amazingly, Catholic religious community is one of the most stable and long-lasting forms of voluntary community in the history of the Western World, even though it lacks a sexual, blood, economic, or political base and is not created with community itself as its objective."

If our coming together is not based on sex, blood, economics, or politics, then what is the basis of our gathering? Simple: the love of Christ and the commitment to the reign of God. Jesus is the great magnet drawing us together. Commitment to his mission is the main expression of our love for him. And so, we can ask ourselves today: What are we incubating—as individuals and as a corporate body? What are we bringing to life with the warmth of our love and faith? How are we inviting the God named Warmth to brood over our bent world with bright wings?

Color Is the Autumn Name of God

Color is one of God's greatest gifts. Ask anyone who has ever gazed upon a crimson rose, the slate-blue sea, a bunch of purple grapes, a bright yellow buttercup, or a yellowish-orangish-pinkish-bluish-purplish sunset. Did you know that the human eye can differentiate seven million colors? We humans can say, therefore, that something is not only blue, but that it is royal blue, powder blue, navy, teal, turquoise, sapphire, cobalt, periwinkle, azure, indigo, or aquamarine. Researchers tell us that color can have a definite effect on our mood and behavior: Babies cry more in yellow rooms, prison inmates are calmer in pink rooms, and people relax better in green rooms.

But what exactly is color? Color originates with light. We perceive sunlight as colorless, as white. But when we hold up a prism to that light, we see that all the colors are present in white light. God's grace is a lot like color. God's grace is pure white, but it comes to us refracted into a wide spectrum of colors. The Vatican Congregation for Institutes of Consecrated Life and Societies of Apostolic Life has published a document entitled *Starting Afresh from Christ*. It says that all consecrated persons must "be formed in the freedom to learn throughout life, in every age and season, in every human ambient and context." We must be open to "any fragment of truth and beauty" found around us. These words reinforce the belief that life itself is the greatest spiritual director. God's grace comes to us through the all the colors that comprise our everyday life. Here is a beautiful little poem that speaks of God's grace.

How to Recognize Grace

It takes you by surprise
It comes in odd packages
It sometimes looks like loss
Or mistakes
It acts like rain
Or like a seed
It's both reliable and unpredictable
It's not what you were aiming at
Or what you thought you deserved
It supplies what you need
Not necessarily what you want
It grows you up
And lets you be a child
It reminds you you're not in control

And that not being in control
is a form of freedom.

Marilyn Chandler McEntyre

"It takes you by surprise." Our God is a God of surprises. When God's grace breaks into our life, we find ourselves saying things like, "What in the world? I didn't expect this." Sometimes God's surprises are delightful and we find ourselves saying "Wow!" Other times, God's surprises appear to be dreadful, and we find ourselves saying "Oh no! Not this!"

Grace "comes in odd packages." That person who gets on my nerves, that line from an old love song, that scent of newly-mown grass, that pouting child, that barking dog, that person who is different from me in ethnic background, language, dress, customs. Yes, grace comes in odd packages. And, guess what, sometimes we are that odd package!

Sometimes grace "looks like loss." The loss of a loved one whose absence colors everything and everywhere and every when, the loss of a cherished ministry, a familiar place, an accustomed way of doing things, the loss of energy, reputation, and memory. Do we trust God enough to believe that even these losses, these dark colors, can be life-giving graces for us?

Sometimes grace looks like "mistakes." In an issue of *Sojourners*, Father Richard Rohr has an article entitled "Beyond Crime and Punishment." It focuses on the scandal of sexual misconduct within our church. In this article, Rohr says that civil law, when dealing with evil, is primarily concerned with crime and punishment. But our Christian faith brings additional dimensions to the problem of wrongdoing—dimensions desperately needed—namely compassion, patience, forgiveness, healing, reconciliation, and transformation. Detecting sin in others can be dangerous, for it can lead us to a sense of self-righteousness or moral superiority which is both non-Christian and lethal. We can find ourselves thinking things like this: "Thank God I'm not a child molester, a liar, a cheat, a druggie." On the contrary, whenever we deal with sin, we must never forget our own solidarity with evil. Rohr writes, "We are all victims and all perpetrators, just in different ways and different times." Father Ray Dlugas, OSA, from the Southdown Institute, says something similar. "Our only hope of integrity as moral teachers and prophets is to speak from a stance of contrite penitents."

Grace "reminds you you're not in control/ And that not being in control is a form of freedom." Our contemporary American culture has it all wrong, doesn't it? It says that freedom is being in control. It says that freedom is doing what I want to do, when I want to do it, and with whom I want to do it. And all along, true freedom was about letting go and allowing God to use us. It is allowing the rainbow of God's grace to transform us into the person of Jesus.

Silence Is the Winter Name of God

Jesus said, "The kingdom of God is among you. It is in your midst." The kingdom of God is already here. At the same time, the kingdom is not yet. It is here in the midst of our human affairs, but it is not always tangible or visible. Fr. Fuellenbach told us we must have a kingdom nose, that is, a big nose that can sniff out the presence of the kingdom in our midst. We must have kingdom ears—big, big ears—to hear the kingdom coming, coming, coming. Yes, Silence is one of God's names. So is Invisibility. So is Powerlessness. How do we help make the kingdom of God more visible? There is only one way: compassion.

The Hebrew word for compassion is rahamin, a word that means "womb." The word compassionate bears the connotation of "wombishness," that is, to love the way a woman loves the child of her womb, the way she nourishes that child with her own life. Compassion is not bending down to the underprivileged from a privileged position. It is walking with others who are suffering and in need, just as Jesus did.

We cannot be compassionate unless we are willing to sacrifice. Patriarch Bartholomew of Constantinople is the spiritual head of the world's Orthodox Christians. He gave an address in Venice in June, as he and Pope John Paul II signed a joint declaration on the environment. The patriarch said: "We often refer to an environmental crisis; but the real crisis lies not in the environment, but in the human heart." He said the only way to solve the environmental crisis is sacrifice, which he defines as "voluntary self-limitation....Only through such self-denial, through our willingness to forgo and to say no or enough will we rediscover our true human place in the universe." He goes on to say that we must "be prepared to make sacrifices that are radical, painful and genuinely unselfish."

The word "sacrifice," though not popular today, must be a part of our personal and communal lexicon. For sacrifice lies at the core of metanoia, that is, conversion or repentance. Someone has said to repent means to change the direction in which you are looking for happiness. Let us ask ourselves these questions: In what areas of my life do I practice voluntary self-limitation? In what areas do I not? Have we as a corporate body made sacrifices that are radical and painful? In which direction am I looking for happiness? Do I need to modify that direction?

Life Is the Spring Name of God

I am reading a book by Barbara Kingsolver entitled *Small Wonder*, a collection of essays she began to write on September 12, 2001. They are her response to September 11. At first glance most of the essays seem a world away from the terrible events of that day, for Kingsolver writes about things like the Grand Canyon, genetic engineering, and her daughter's chicken coop. But in the introduction, Kingsolver explains: "I believe our largest problems have grown from the earth's remotest corners as well as our own backyards, and that salvation may lie in those places too."

She begins her book with a story from the Lorena Province of Iran. A sixteen-month-old boy wandered away from his teenage babysitter while the boy's parents were working in the wheat field. When his parents learn he is missing, they are filled with anguish. Fearing the worst, they search everywhere for their little boy for several days. He is nowhere to be found. Eventually the father and several other men go into the mountains a few miles away and begin to search inside the caves. They happen into a dark cave and find the boy alive and well, cradled in the arms of a mother bear who has been feeding him with her own milk.

I love this story! And I ask: Who are we in this story? Perhaps we are the frantic parents, filled with anguish because we have lost someone utterly precious. Perhaps we are frantically searching and banging our fists on the door of hope. Or maybe we are the teenage babysitter, consumed with guilt and shame for having allowed someone so precious to slip through our fingers. Or maybe we're the little boy, wandering off, lured by a flitting butterfly or a flitting anything—whatever draws us away from the shelter of family, friends, community, church.

But I like to think that most of all we are the mother bear! We are filled with the milk of God's word, God's love, God's compassion. After all, it was Saint Julian of Norwich who said something like this: We drink milk from the breast of our tender Mother Jesus! Only a mystic could get away with saying such a shocking thing: breast? milk? Mother Jesus? For we who are not mystics know that Jesus was male. And we know there are strict boundaries between being male and female, just as there are strict boundaries between everything: male/female, young/old, Christian/Jew/Muslim, liberal/conservative, gay/straight, third world/first world, chickens/kittens, bears/humans! But this story presents us with a kinder universe, a more mystical one in which boundaries are not so rigid, so exclusive, so absolute. A world where the lion lies down with the lamb, where there is neither Gentile/Jew, man/woman, free/slave any more, a world where justice prevails and compassion runs riot.

What is your name for God? Is it Warmth, Color, Silence, Life? In all of this, we must remember Jesus' name for God was Abba, the one who loves us unconditionally, forgives us absolutely, and is with us always. My prayer for all of us is that we too continue to experience this daily Abba, this close and nurturing parent, this Father/Mother God. And may this experience free us more and more to follow in the footsteps of the compassionate Jesus with integrity, eagerness, and great, great joy!

❧ *What struck me in this chapter? Why?*

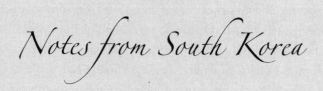

CHAPTER 19

Notes from South Korea

In September 2002, I spent a month in South Korea attending an international meeting of the Sisters of Notre Dame. The conference was held at the provincial center of the Sisters of Notre Dame in Inchon near Seoul. Here are some facts I learned about Korea upon my arrival:

- Seoul has been the capital of Korea for 600 years.

- Seoul, with its ten million people, is the fifth-largest city in the world.

- Seventy percent of Korea is made up of mountains.

- Land in Korea sells for $5,000 a square yard.

- The Koreans had metal, movable type 200 years before Europe did.

- The sisters have indoor and outdoor shoes. In some of the rooms in the house they wear no shoes.

- There are 800 priests in Seoul. We met one who was forty-nine years old. He ranks 149th in age, which means there are 650 priests younger than he is.

One day we visited the Demilitarized Zone (DMZ), the 155-mile border (about two miles wide) between North and South Korea that has existed for over fifty years. It is a "no man's land." Only one small village exists within the zone and those villagers have a strict curfew. We had to receive special permission to visit the DMZ. Before being driven into the zone, we had to sign a waiver not holding the U.N. or anyone else liable if we were injured or killed while there. That was sobering! We also had to agree to a strict dress code—no jeans or shorts (no problem for us!)—and to obey all the rules: no stopping when walking, no picture taking at certain places, no pointing or gesturing which could be interpreted by the North Korean soldiers as mockery. The young U.S. soldier who was our guide was a lanky and articulate young man from Texas.

We visited the actual room where the truce was signed in 1953, and where negotiations between the North and the South continue to take place. The DMZ line runs right through the middle of the table! We stopped at a few guard towers along the way and gazed across into North Korea. At one point, we prayed for peace together and sang "Dona Nobis Pacem." One of our Korean sisters then publicly thanked the sisters from the United States for the sacrifice of human life our country made during the Korean War. Over 142,000 American soldiers were killed in Korea, a number that astounds me.

The DMZ is an eerie place. There are buildings, but no human beings. It looks like a ghost town. Ironically, the DMZ has turned into a marvelous nature preserve since no humans disturb it. There are birds, plants, and animals in the zone that are not found anywhere else in Korea. So, in one small way, good has come from a very terrible situation. At the end of our tour, the young soldier asked if he could have his picture taken with us. "I've never been with so many nuns before," he said, "and I'd like to send the picture home to my mother." We obliged him, of course.

We had a special holy hour on September 11, to pray for the United States and for world peace. It began in our dimmed chapel with Sister Sujita, our Superior General, striking a Buddhist gong eleven times. Every eleven minutes she rang it again. In between we sang a few songs, listened to Scripture readings in five languages, and prayed in silence.

Near the provincial house where I stayed was some sort of a monastery. Every day on a regular basis I could hear one of the monks yelling (literally) his prayers to God. Across from this monastery was a South Korean military installation. Every day on a regular basis I heard the bang-bang of rifles as the soldiers practiced their shooting. What a contrast: that lone monk hurling his prayers to the heavens, and the steady bang-bang of those rifles. I called these two sounds my "auditory icon of our age." What a fitting background for us here at this conference to discuss and to pray for world peace!

Inchon is a huge modern city. At night it is ablaze with neon lights. As we drove through the city one night, I thought, "This is one of the prettiest cities I have ever seen." Then I realized why it was so beautiful: I couldn't read the Korean words of those neon lights! I was not distracted by such signs as "Kim's Fish Market" or "Eat at Joe's." I saw only lovely colors, shapes, and lines.

A few miscellaneous observations:

- Most of the bus drivers in Korea wear white gloves. If you carry up the offertory gifts at Mass, you also wear white gloves.

- I like the politeness of the Korean people. Even the maintenance man bows deeply to me when I pass him in the hall.

- *Saranghaeyo* means "I love you."

- I continue to eat things I have never eaten before, like water lily stems (delicious!).

- One of the Korean sisters did a little acupuncture on my hands and neck, without needles. It felt wonderful!

- *Anyonghee gaseyo* means goodbye.

- Sometimes at Mass we all said the Our Father aloud simultaneously in our own language. How beautiful it was to hear the prayer being said in eight different languages at the same time.

- I liked weighing myself in kilos. (Remember, one kilo is 2.2 pounds!)

One weekend we had a wonderful excursion into Korean history and culture. Our first stop was the shrine of the Korean martyrs. The stained glass windows, altar, and tabernacle at the shrine were all designed by our Korean sister, Sister Theresita. I learned there were 103 martyrs, all canonized on the same day by Pope John Paul II when he visited Korea in 1984. Catholicism was brought to Korea from China by lay catechists, not by priests. The father of one of the martyrs was taught his catechism by Saint Julie Billiart in Amiens, France.

For me the highlight of our trip was our two-hour visit to a Buddhist seminary for women. The seminary, which houses 250 students, is a large compound with about twenty-five buildings nestled in a valley amid many pine trees. We were greeted at the gate by our guide, a monk named the Only Truth. She has been a professor at the seminary since she graduated twenty-six years ago. She was about forty-eight years old with shaven head and wearing a gray robe with long, wide sleeves. She had a broad smile, expressive eyes, and greeted us warmly with, "Today we have special guests!" We were permitted to enter the compound because we were religious sisters. Then Only Truth showed us around, pointing out to us a 500-year-old weeping pine tree, the lecture hall, the library (with Internet access), and the meditation hall. I was a little surprised to spot one student using a pay phone. I also saw a wall with about 250 cubicles. A glass and a toothbrush were in each cubicle.

The seminary course of studies lasts four years. The young women at the seminary live a very disciplined life. They rise at 3 AM for prayer and eat all their meals in silence. They spend many hours each day in classes, at prayer, or studying. They also have assigned chores. I saw some preparing the noonday meal while others were trimming bushes. A sense of calm and peace reigned wherever we went.

Eventually we were taken to the tea room where some of the students served us tea, rice cakes, and grapes. At one point Only Truth commented that Catholic sisters have much in common with Buddhist monks. "We are all women devoted to discovering the truth and to living virtuously," she said simply. She also spoke about the importance of compassion and love. When it was time to leave, we sang a song for her and the students: "Ubi Caritas" in three part harmony. The moment was picture perfect—the tea, the rice cakes, the sitting together on the floor, the oriental garden right outside the open windows. I felt so united with these women and with God. As Only Truth walked us back to the gate, she spoke about the current dialogue between Catholic nuns and Buddhist monks, and how wonderful it was. I was proud to learn that some of our Korean sisters are part of this dialogue.

Another day we visited Bakmum School, the only school our Korean sisters own. It is an all girls' school with 2,000 students from grades seven to twelve. We were welcomed with tea and cakes and then shown a PowerPoint presentation (in English) of the school's history. Next we were escorted to the classes we had signed up for. Sister Sujita and I went to a second-year English class with thirty students. The girls applauded when we entered the room. They were excited that sisters from all over the world were visiting their school. They asked their questions in English: "Where are you from? What is your country like? Do you have Baskin-Robbins in your country?"

Afterward we went to the auditorium where the students performed for us. One girl played the Korean flute, another sang a traditional song, and a teacher danced. But the most unusual performance was done by a group of twelve girls, each with a drum or gong. They processed onto the stage, sat down quietly, and then, right on cue, began to furiously pound their drums in perfect unison. It was the loudest drum playing I have ever heard. An explosion of noise! They whacked away at the drums and gongs in various cadences for a full twenty minutes. It was incredible!

One more incident touched me very much. About six of us visited a home for elderly women which our sisters run. The house, donated to our sisters for this work, is nestled in the heart of the city amid stores, businesses, and skyscrapers. One sister lives in the house with nine women. A cook and several volunteers help her. The elderly ladies were thrilled to see us. The first woman I met, Elizabeth, was eighty-seven—the same age as my mother. When, through an interpreter, I told her she was my mother's age, she gave me a big hug, her little head coming up to my chest.

Sunday we went to Seoul, a huge city nestled between mountains along the beautiful Han River. We went to the top of a huge tower and got a breathtaking glimpse of the vast city below. We then visited the first house our German sisters purchased when they came to Korea in 1967. Sixteen sisters live here now and are involved in eleven ministries including a day care center and a training center for catechists. We also visited the Cathedral in Seoul. Mass is celebrated virtually every hour there on Sundays, and all of the Masses are packed.

Being in Korea has given me a taste of what it's like to be "illiterate." I not only cannot read Korean words, I cannot read even the letters. I walk into a library and see 22,000 volumes, but I can't read a single one of them! It's both frustrating and humbling. I appreciate what it feels like to be illiterate.

Being in Korea has also given me the experience of "sticking out." Obviously, I am not Korean. I look different. The other day a group of kindergartners walked by us, and one little girl pointed at us and yelled something. When I asked one of our Korean sisters what the little girl had said, she replied, "Look! Foreigners!" So this experience of being an obvious "foreigner" has heightened my awareness of what "foreigners" in any country experience.

The international conference was a wonderful experience for me, and being in Korea was an extra blessing.

❧ *Did I learn anything new about Korea from this chapter? How have I been enriched by different cultures or countries?*

CHAPTER 20

Border Crossings

When I returned from Korea, I happened to find the latest issue of *Weavings* on my desk. In it was an article entitled "Border Crossings" by Deborah Smith Douglas, an Episcopal laywoman. This article not only resonated with my experience of visiting the Demilitarized Zone in Korea, it inspired me to dedicate this reflection to the borders in our lives and God's call to cross over.

On the human level, borders are significant places. To cross a border—whether it be a doorway, a gate, a river, or a line drawn in the sand—can be frightening or exhilarating. Many of us can remember the first time we were allowed to leave the confines of our own yard or to cross the street by ourselves. One memorable border experience from my childhood happened when I was about eight. My family went to Niagara Falls, and I remember the thrill of standing on the Peace Bridge with one foot in Canada and the other in the United States.

Scripture is filled with stories of more serious border crossings. At the prompting of God, Abraham left the security of his native land and journeyed across many borders into the land of Canaan. The Hebrews, under Moses' leadership, crossed the boundary of the Red Sea in their quest for freedom. Years later, their descendants crossed the Jordan River into the Promised Land. In our own day we regularly hear poignant stories of refugees from Mexico jeopardizing their lives to cross the border into the United States, or Haitians risking death on the open sea to enter our shores. These crossings, as daring as they are, pale in comparison to the great border crossing that lies at the heart of our Christian faith: the Incarnation. As Douglas says, at the Annunciation, God through Mary, "stepped over the line not only between heaven and earth, but between divinity and humanity."

Unfortunately we can take the mystery of the Incarnation for granted. As the writer Brennan Manning has said, we fail to "quake at the inbreak of God Almighty." We "rob Christmas of its shock value." We "trivialize the divine scandal into gingerbread creches." Father Ronald Rolheiser, in *The Holy Longing*, says something similar when he describes the Incarnation as the "most under-understood" mystery of our faith. He claims we tend to reduce the Incarnation to something that happened 2,000 years ago and only to the person of Jesus. But, he says, the Incarnation was not a thirty-three year experiment nor was it a one-shot deal. Rather, the Incarnation of Jesus continues through all time and in all people. The season of Advent encourages us to reflect on and give thanks for this incredible gift.

> ❧ *What border crossings have I experienced in my life? Is there any evidence that I trivialize the Incarnation? Do I really believe Jesus is incarnate in all people? If so, how does this belief affect my behavior?*

During his earthly ministry, Jesus gave abundant evidence that he was a radical border crosser. He crossed the borders of convention by freely associating with all people: men and women, Jew and Gentile, rich and poor, sick and healthy. He allowed no boundaries—physical, psychological, self-protective—to divide him from the people he came to serve nor to separate him from Abba's will. Jesus constantly challenged his followers to cross borders. "Love one another," he said over and over again, fully aware that love longs for divisions to end and barriers to fall down. At the Last Supper, he said, "Do this in remembrance of me" (Lk 22:19). These words refer not only to the celebration of the Eucharist. They also refer to the sum total of Jesus' teachings and his personal way of living— especially laying down his life for us. We who claim to be disciples of Jesus must be border crossers too.

What borders are we called to cross? There are many. The borders can be exterior, interior, or a mixture of both. Sometimes, for example, we play life safe. We "stay at home," clinging to the security of what is known and familiar. We find ourselves saying things like: "This is the way I've always done it. I'm too old to change now. That's not my responsibility." Or an unseen line can separate us from a new ministry, a new experience, a new relationship, a new way of looking at something. When Jesus invites us to "Do this," he may be saying: "Come to the edge of what you know and go beyond it. Come to the brink of the chasm that separates you from this thing and jump across. Trust me, I'll be with you!"

One of the most fortified borders in our contemporary world is, of course, the border that separates the rich from the poor, the haves from the have nots. This border is hard to cross for it is often patrolled by fear, prejudice, ignorance, convention, or apathy. Jesus continually invites us to cross this boundary and to enter into the lives of the poor, the needy, the sick, the unattractive, or simply the different from us.

❧ *Have I erected borders between myself and those who are poor and needy? What concrete steps can I take toward crossing one of these borders?*

One quality that encourages border crossings is the gift of empathy. Monika Hellwig, in her book *Guests of God*, speaks of empathy on terms of a crossing over. She writes, "The human capacity for empathy (is) the ability to cross over on a kind of bridge of imagination into the experience of another person." With empathy, we can recognize cruelty, because we can imagine the pain and suffering of the other. Similarly, we know what kindness is because we can imagine the joy and pleasure of the other.

Empathy is vital to our Christian life for yet another reason; it enables us to think in terms of community. Says Hellwig, empathy helps us "to say 'we' and thereby capture a concept capable of indefinite expansion to embrace others." This ability to think in terms of community or the common good is essential for the well-being of our life on planet earth. As Hellwig reminds us, "Any quest for personal happiness that is not a quest for the common good has no hope of ultimate success."

❧ *When have I been moved by empathy lately? Think of someone who is separated from me by some significant chasm. What could help me to build a bridge over this chasm?*

Jesus crossed over the great divide by becoming human. But through his resurrection, he "crossed an even greater frontier, breaking through the bounds of death itself, going before us into life everlasting, enabling us to follow him" (Douglas, *Weavings*). Recently, in one of the other provinces, a sister lay dying in the health care center. A number of sisters went into her room to pray for her and to say their final goodbyes. One of her best friends leaned over her and, with tears in her eyes, whispered, "I'll see you again on the other side." On the other side. What a meaningful expression of the continuity of life. What a beautiful testimony to belief in the Resurrection. As the theologian Jungen Moltmann has said, "To believe means to cross in hope...the bounds that have been penetrated by the raising of the Crucified."

This is a good time to ask ourselves: Why do we allow ourselves to be confined by borders? Why do we hesitate to grow, to change, to reach out, to move forward? I suspect it is not so much that we lack courage as it is that we lack love. By love, I do not mean some warm and fuzzy feeling. By love I mean hard work, the hard work of being attentive and open to others who are different from us or who disturb or frighten us; the hard work of continuing to love even after we have suffered misunderstanding, betrayal, failure, or loss; the hard work of doing not only the good thing, but the most loving thing.

During the past few years, I have been inspired by the border crossings I have witnessed in my province and in individual sisters. I am heartened, for example, by the bridge that has been built between the sisters and our lay associates. I am encouraged by the collaboration I have seen among the four U.S. provinces. I take heart when I see sisters from four different provinces from the United States and Germany ministering side by side in Uganda. I am equally edified when I see individual sisters making themselves available for demanding ministries, achieving incredible results in ministry despite limited resources, negotiating painful transitions in their lives with remarkable grace, or facing death, the final border crossing, with faith and courage.

My prayer for all of us is a simple one.

Jesus, Incarnate One,
    you stand at the edge of our borders,
    the lines we have drawn with such deliberation,
    the walls we have built with such fear.
You say, "Cross over!"
We say, "I can't! I'm too afraid…too old…too busy…too tired."
You say, "Nonsense! Come! I will be with you!"

Loving Jesus,
    help us be border crossers like you.
Help us move freely from here to there,
    using the bridge of our imagination
    to empathize with others,
        especially those who are poor and needy.
Give us strength to do the hard work of real loving.
Give us courage to invite others into the sacred space of who we are.
And when death, the final border crossing, comes,
    may we step, skip, dance, run, or tumble joyfully
    into the other side of the wholeness of your love.
Amen.

CHAPTER 21

Celibacy and Homelessness

The season of Lent is an opportune time to reflect on celibacy. The impetus for choosing the topic of celibacy came from an experience I had at the Korean Conference. One day the sisters were discussing the chapter on consecrated chastity in the new draft of our constitutions. We noticed that the new draft omitted the reference to celibacy as a renunciation of marriage and family. Evidently some sisters felt that such a reference was "too negative." After all, celibacy entails much more than a "giving up." Although I could understand their point, I spoke out in favor of keeping the aspect of renunciation in our constitutions. I said something like this: "It is not healthy for us to gloss over the very real renunciations we have made by making a vow of chastity. The stark reality is that we all sleep alone."

I want to offer a few thoughts here about consecrated celibacy including the aspect of renunciation. These reflections can be helpful to Christians in all states of life. I base some of my remarks on the book, *Selling All*, by Sandra Schneiders, IHM, especially the section on "Celibacy and Home." I will begin with Jesus and the concept of homelessness.

Celibacy and Homelessness

Tradition tells us that Jesus lived two very different lifestyles. For the first thirty years of his life he lived a stable, private, hidden life in the home of his parents. At age thirty or so, he suddenly undertook a short public life characterized by mobility and itinerancy. As he said, "Foxes have holes, and birds of the air have nests; but the Son of Man has nowhere to lay his head" (Lk 9:58). During the period of his public life, Jesus had two distinct types of disciples: those who were called to share his itinerant way of life (for example, the apostles) and those who were not called to do so (followers such as Lazarus, Mary, and Martha). Schneiders refers to these two forms of discipleship as homelessness and householding. She sees both as equal and complementary.

By professing vows of chastity, poverty, and obedience, apostolic women religious embrace the first kind of discipleship, the discipleship of homelessness. Although all three vows impact homelessness, I will mention only the vow of celibacy here. By celibacy we religious pledge to invest our whole heart in our relationship with Jesus in a way that excludes any other primary commitment. In starker terms this means we have no lover(s), and we freely forgo marriage, children, and establishing a place to call our own. Making such a vow is risky business. Why? Because most individuals attain maturity precisely through a commitment to a partner, the founding of a family, and the establishment of a home. By renouncing these things, we risk perpetual immaturity—unless our celibacy frees us to love passionately and broadly. Joan Chittister, OSB, writes, "Chastity is love given with an open hand....(It) is love poured out, pressed down and overflowing. Passionate it is; clinging it isn't." Consecrated chastity allows Jesus and the gospel to be the central core and driving force of our lives.

Even in little ways we are reminded of our itinerancy in following Christ. We may not live in the house of our choosing. We may not get the room we want or the carpet we would like. We don't get to pick our neighbors either. Ask the sisters in our health care center about homelessness, and they will probably tell you that, as beautiful as their rooms are (and they are beautiful!), the rooms are only a temporary stopping off place on their journey of faith, until God calls them to their final and permanent home: heaven.

Celibacy, Homelessness, and Community

We live our homelessness within a community. Herein lies a paradox. While community can supply many of the affective resources we need as mature women, it can never substitute for the family we left or the family we will never begin. Sometimes we put too much of a demand on our religious community to meet all our affective needs. When we find ourselves saying in disgust, "This community!" we may really be saying, "I'm lonely! I'm scared! I feel misunderstood! I'm not getting my way!" How much more honest it is to admit these things rather than blame our sisters for not being the partner we don't have, the children and grandchildren we freely renounced, or the home of our own that would give us a certain security and independence.

In his book *Sing a New Song*, Timothy Radcliffe, OP, tells the story of a disillusioned novice who, after several months in the novitiate, complained to his novice director about the selfish and petty Dominicans he was encountering in community. His director said, "I am delighted to hear that you no longer admire us. Now there is a chance that you might come to love us." The redemptive mystery of God's goodness is seen not in a community of perfect persons, but in a community of flawed and injured persons who, despite their imperfections, encourage and support one another in their common journey of faith. This acceptance of human sinfulness reminds me of a line from "The Rock" by T.S. Eliot when he speaks of people who are "dreaming of systems so perfect that no one will need to be good." Or, as Father Zosima says in *The Brothers Karamazov*, "Love in practice is a hard and dreadful thing compared to love in dreams."

At the same time, our sinfulness is no excuse for neglecting to cherish the persons who share our commitment. We can ask ourselves, how do I help provide for the affective needs of others in my local community and in my congregation? As provincial, I was very happy when I heard that profession groups were getting together for supper, sisters were meeting to discuss a book, or two sisters had met to talk about their differences. Such encounters encourage the healthy intimacy we all need and desire.

Celibacy, Homelessness, and Friendship

Because of our celibacy, we religious have a unique opportunity to witness to a kind of love that is non-sexual and non-possessive, namely friendship. Jesus developed this kind of relationship with his followers and encouraged them to develop it among themselves. In the words of Schneiders, "Religious are not non-relational nomads tangentially brushing or occasionally colliding with other nomads. Nor are they a corps of workers on the march with eyes so fixed on the goal that they do not see one another or the people to whom they are sent." Rather, religious and all Christians should enjoy a life that is richly relational, with all relationships radiating outward from the primary relationship with Jesus.

I know from personal experience how important friendship is. I also know how easy it is for me to be consumed by my work and to be identified by my title. Once when I was provincial, I ran into two Jesuits at a meeting. I knew both of them from my days in Detroit. When they saw me, they greeted me with an enthusiastic "Melannie!" and a warm hug. I was almost embarrassed by how much their affection meant to me. Later when I reflected on the incident, I found myself saying, "Why were you embarrassed by your need for friendship and affection? Instead of apologizing for this need, thank God you were reminded of it today—and in such a pleasant way!"

Celibacy, Homelessness, and World Peace

At this moment our world is beset with wars and violence of all kinds. Celibate homelessness has great potential for fostering in us a spirituality of non-violence, a spirituality of peace. By our vows, we have renounced participation for our own profit from the economic, political, and social dynamics of our world. This renunciation flows not from a contempt for the world, but from a profound reverence for the world as God's sacred creation. We religious above all should see the God-infused character of all creation. As Schneiders writes: "Religious are called to be citizens of whatever place they inhabit, children of the cosmos who do not recognize any absolute claims except those of God and hence can transcend the artificial boundaries humans have introduced to divide up land, resources, peoples, and even religion itself." If we look at the current global crisis, we see that those "artificial boundaries" have led us into war, a war which is having devastating consequences for our entire planet.

Women religious have been in the forefront of the peace movement—and rightfully so. As an international congregation, my community is in a unique position to witness collaboration that transcends national borders and particular cultures. All of us might ask ourselves, what am I doing to foster peace in my local community, my workplace, my country, my world?

On Ash Wednesday, we hear the sober words, "Turn away from sin and be faithful to the gospel." Let us embrace anew the homelessness we see exemplified by Jesus. Let us continue to invest our whole hearts in our relationship with Jesus, and consciously make choices that nourish friendship—especially with one another. Let us work untiringly to remove those artificial boundaries that divide us. Let us do these things, confident that Jesus himself is our itinerant traveling companion, leading us to love as Jesus loves without distinction, qualification, or limit.

❧ *What is the connection between celibacy, homelessness, and world peace?*

CHAPTER 22

I Have Never Seen the Face of God

I have never seen the face of God.
No angel ever came to me.
I have never witnessed a miracle,
  a blind man see,
  a bent woman stand straight and tall,
  a dead girl sit up and cry, "I'm hungry,"
    or 5,000 people fed by two fish and five loaves of bread.
But I have tasted strawberries.
I have smelled bread baking, and I drank cool water
  and rich, red wine.
I have been lifted up by a robin's chirp,
  and been humbled by the stars and ocean.
I have planted seeds, pulled weeds, washed clothes, typed letters,
  waited in line, asked questions, given my opinion, picketed.
I have attended meetings, read great books, sung in church,
  played cards, talked to squirrels, made repairs, danced the polka.
I have cradled a newborn in my arms and kept vigil with the dying.
  I have fallen exhausted into bed at night
    and risen again in the morning.
I have said, "I'm sorry…I forgive…Thank you…I don't know."

I have held someone I love,

  and I have been held by someone who loves me.

I have won and lost, known sickness and health, ecstasy and dread.

And through it all,

  God is the one who is always present.

  God as companion, stranger, hunger, goad.

  God as lover, friend, tag-along, intruder, foe.

  God as answer and as question, blinding light and dark abyss.

  God, God, God.

 ❧ *What are some of the ways I encounter God in my everyday life?*

CHAPTER 23

The Sacredness of Creation

Recently I finished reading the book, *When the Trees Say Nothing*, edited by Kathleen Deignan. The book is a collection of Thomas Merton's writings on nature. In it, Merton writes on such things as the four seasons, birds, flowers, trees, cattle, deer, bugs, snakes, clouds, mountains, and stars. The book resonated with my own love for nature, a love acquired as a little girl traipsing around the pastures and woods of our small farm. Merton's writings, coupled with my own experience of nature, has prompted me to devote this reflection to nature and the indispensable role it plays in our spiritual lives.

We can begin by posing the question: What is the relationship between nature and the spiritual life? In his book *The Re-Enchantment of Everyday Life*, Thomas Moore states this: "Nature is the prime source of the spiritual life. Block it out, and we obliterate the source of the spirit that the soul thrives on." Thomas Berry echoes these sentiments when he writes, "The natural world [is] the primary manifestation of the divine to human intelligence." As believers, we reverence nature as a reflection of the God we have come to know as good. For us, creation is sacred.

This sense of the sacredness of creation is the basis of conservation. As Thomas Berry has said, "We will not save what we do not love. And we will neither love nor save what we do not experience as sacred." We might ask ourselves, what are some ways we can grow in our appreciation of the sacredness of creation?

Doing Nothing

One way to appreciate the sacredness of creation is simply by taking the time to observe and to be with nature. We can do this in many ways: by taking a leisurely walk, gazing out a window, listening to the rain, watching the birds, looking up at the stars, fingering the bark of a tree, smelling a sprig of lilac, biting into an apple, petting a puppy, reading up on owls, or even watching a nature show on television. John Henry Newman, for all his scholarly brilliance and intense activity, loved animals. Even as an elderly cardinal, he would regularly take the train into London to spend a day at the zoo. Perhaps we could all profit by a visit to a local zoo or to an arboretum, aviary, conservatory, or park. I sense we would be healthier women and men if we carved out a few minutes each day to do nothing, that is, to do nothing except observe and be with one tiny segment of the incredibly fascinating world pulsating around and in us.

When I am on retreat or enjoying my day off, I, like many of you, take longer periods of time to do nothing except observe nature. Sometimes I allow myself the luxury of jotting down some of my observations and seeing where these observations take me. Once when I was at our vacation house, I came upon a goose nest in the back yard by the lake. I wrote this reflection.

> I curiously and cautiously went over and peeked into the nest. I saw four beautiful goose eggs nestled in a bed of soft down. How could anyone not be moved by such a sight? The perfectly formed eggs…the down plucked from the goose's own breast…the goslings developing unseen inside the shells…the devotion of the female to sit on those eggs for six long weeks…the courage of the gander to fend off predators. When I got into bed last night, I couldn't stop thinking about that nest with those four precious eggs.

Fasting from Technology

We live in a world steeped in technology. We take for granted inventions such as light bulbs, cars, airplanes, telephones, TVs, computers, microwaves, DVD players. Although technology can certainly be a blessing, it can also be a distraction. Sometimes it distracts and distances us from the natural world. We can sit in front of a computer screen, for example, instead of going for a walk in the woods. We can watch TV instead of planting a few flowers. We can buy processed foods to pop into the microwave instead of cutting up carrots, boiling rice, or mashing potatoes.

Father John Staudenmaier, SJ, has written extensively on the positive and negative impact of modern technology on humanity. When he gives talks, he often invites people to abstain from technology for twenty-four hours. That means no radio, no TV, no phone, no computer, no microwave, no car. If that is impossible to do, he encourages people at least to do without light bulbs for a day or so. What is the purpose? First, voluntary fasting can give us a greater appreciation of technology. But it does more than that. Fasting from light bulbs can help us to appreciate the beauty, power, and mystery of darkness. It helps us to see darkness not merely as the absence of light, but as a marvelous entity in and of itself. Fasting from technology can also bring us a greater appreciation of silence. It can slow life down for us.

When I lived in my own apartment in Detroit, I tried fasting from technology occasionally. I remember how quiet the apartment became. I found myself becoming aware of the steady humming of the refrigerator, a sound I had not noticed because of all the other noises in my life. (No, I did not unplug my refrigerator.) I discovered that walking to church was less of a hassle than driving and searching for a parking place in the crowded lot. In the evening, I found the candlelight soothing. And because it was so dark so soon, I went to bed earlier than I ordinarily would have.

Contemplating nature and fasting from technology are not religious acts in themselves. But they can become religious acts if they lead to a change of heart. In 1991, in *Renewing the Earth*, the U.S. Catholic bishops called us to a change of heart with these sobering words: "The environmental crisis of our own day constitutes an exceptional call to conversion….As individuals, as institutions, as a people, we need a change of heart to save the planet for our children and generations yet unborn." When we take the time to contemplate nature, we not only get in touch with God's bounty, we also learn how we might become better stewards of God's bounty. When we fast from artificial light, we not only save electricity, we also discover those urgings of God that come to us only under the cover of darkness.

War affects God's creation. Right now, a terrible war is waging in Iraq. I am reminded of what a young college woman said at a prayer gathering for peace I attended a few weeks ago. She noted that when the war broke out in Sarajevo, all the birds left and didn't return until the fighting stopped. Imagine a place devoid of all birds! I wonder what other aspects of the natural world (including human life) were disrupted or destroyed by that war? I like to think that if we humans were truly aware of the sacredness of those birds (and, by extension, the sacredness of all creation), perhaps those guns would never have been fired in the first place.

The Challenge of Easter

Joan Chittister, OSB, says that we miss the point of Easter if we reduce it "to an historical event rather than a life-changing commitment." She writes, "To celebrate Easter means to stand in the light of the empty tomb and decide what to do next." My prayer for all of us is this: May we make time to contemplate God's creation wherever we are. May our contemplation lead us to a greater realization of the sacredness of creation. And may this realization cause us to decide what to do next with our lives.

❧ *What part does creation play in my spiritual life? How do I make time to contemplate God's creation wherever I may be?*

CHAPTER 24

In Praise of Vulnerability

The first Pentecost was an exciting event. The Holy Spirit showed up in the upper room in a rather dramatic way, complete with special effects of howling wind, fiery tongues, and inspired speech. In reading the description of that amazing event, we might be tempted to think that the only way the Spirit breaks into our lives is through the extraordinary. Such an interpretation would be misleading, however, for Scripture makes it clear that, although God sometimes employs the extraordinary to communicate with humankind, God's usual mode of communicating with us is precisely through the ordinary.

In fact, Scripture goes even further and says that God often chooses to break into our lives not merely through the extraordinary or ordinary, but even through the under-ordinary! In other words, God has a predilection for showing up amid pain, poverty, and powerlessness. Isn't this what Mary sings in her Magnificat? "He has filled the hungry with good things, and sent the rich away empty" (Lk 1:53). Isn't this what Jesus describes in the Beatitudes? "Blessed are you who are poor, for yours is the kingdom of God" (Lk 6:20). Isn't this what Saint Paul says in the letter to the Corinthians? "For whenever I am weak, then I am strong" (2 Cor 12:10).

Vulnerability

I would like to share a few reflections on the concept of vulnerability and the key role it plays in our spiritual lives. We can begin by asking what exactly is vulnerability? The Pulitzer Prize-winning biography, *Lindbergh*, by A. Scott Berg offers one answer. The book describes the terrible tragedy that befell Charles and Anne Lindbergh when their one-year-old baby, Charlie Jr., was kidnapped from his nursery one night and was killed. Anne's response to this devastating loss was a period of intense grieving. For months she was deeply depressed and often burst into tears whether alone or with her family. Charles' response, in sharp contrast, was a stoic one. Throughout the ordeal he kept a stiff upper lip. Years later Anne made this astute observation about her husband's stoicism: "Stoicism is a shield, permissible for a short time only. In the end, one has to discard shields and remain open and vulnerable. Otherwise, scar tissue will seal off the wound and no growth will follow. To grow, to be reborn, one must remain vulnerable—open to love but also hideously open to the possibility of more suffering."

I can resonate with these words. Vulnerability means to be open to love. At the same time, it means to be "hideously open" to the possibility of more suffering. Some of us, after experiencing severe pain and suffering, erect a shield around ourselves in an attempt to prevent more suffering. Unfortunately, by doing so, we can cut ourselves off from growth and rebirth. We can even jeopardize God's saving action in our lives and, by extension, in the world.

> ❧ *How have I experienced God's presence in the extraordinary, the ordinary, the under-ordinary? Have I ever assumed a stoic stance in response to pain and suffering?*

The Vulnerable Jesus

Vulnerability is the hallmark of Jesus' life. The Incarnation itself is a paradigm of vulnerability. That the almighty and infinite God should assume human form with all its limitations is nothing short of incredible. As the writer Brennan Manning says, "God entered into our world not with the crushing impact of unbearable glory, but in the way of weakness, vulnerability, and need."

Throughout his earthly life, Jesus remained completely vulnerable. He eagerly entered into relationships, thus risking misunderstanding and betrayal. He openly spoke the truth, thus risking criticism and condemnation. He continuously reached out in love to women, children, Gentiles, the sick, and the poor, thus risking the wrath of the religious and political leaders of his day. When it became clear that his enemies were out to silence him once and for all, Jesus did not retract his words, curb his behavior, nor slink into hiding. Rather, he boldly turned his face toward Jerusalem and met his executioners with amazing courage and calm. Perhaps there is no greater evidence of Jesus' vulnerability than when he hung naked and dying on the cross.

The heart of Jesus' vulnerability, however, was not his courage. It was the extent of his unselfish love. Jesus' life and teachings are diametrically opposed to Satan, the father of lies. Satan says this to humankind: "You will find happiness by focusing on yourself, by dominating others, by controlling your future, by accumulating material goods." What a contrast to these lies are the words and example of Jesus: "You will find happiness by focusing on others, by spending your life in unselfish service of others, by entrusting your future to God, by sharing and giving away your material goods."

❧ *What evidence is there in my life that I believe Satan or I believe Jesus? What evidence is there in our life that we as a family, parish, or religious community believe Satan or believe Jesus?*

Forms of Vulnerability

Vulnerability takes many forms. One form is diminishment. We can experience diminishment both as individuals and as a community. As individuals, we all experience the gradual diminishment of the aging process. As a middle-aged sister once said to me, "This morning as I stumbled out of bed, I found myself asking, 'When did I get my mother's body?'" We experience our diminishment corporately, too. During my term as provincial, I officiated at the funerals of over sixty sisters. I saw my province membership decrease to under 400 sisters for the first time since 1928.

When we experience diminishment, we may become fearful or even angry. That's exactly when we must resist the temptation to place our hope in power and numbers. In her book *Finding the Treasure*, Sandra Schneiders talks about the drastic decrease in membership of apostolic congregations within the past twenty years. She says, "It is highly unlikely that very large numbers of people are actually, or ever were, called to religious life. A lifelong commitment to consecrated celibacy, which is at the heart of the vocation to religious life, is not the 'normal' path to Christian holiness." Because of the large numbers of women who flocked to religious life in the 1940s, '50s, and early '60s, we have a "falsely inflated image of what a healthy religious congregation looks like."

Schneiders dares to say that religious communities do not need large numbers of members. She notes that many contemplative communities that have been in existence for hundreds of years have never had more than a dozen members. Unlike many apostolic congregations, contemplative communities are not pressured by the felt need for workers to staff institutions or to earn money. "They are basically about the business of being religious." Schneiders concludes with these words: "Religious life needs only as many people as are called to it because it does not exist to produce some specific product." As we experience diminishment on all levels, it is good to remind ourselves that, throughout human history, God seems to work best through the few and the weak, not the many and the strong.

> ❧ *How am I experiencing diminishment on a personal level? Do I really believe God often works best through the few and the weak?*

Other forms of vulnerability are fatigue and uncertainty. If we are true to our Christian vocation whether it be as religious, as spouses and/or parents, or as single Christians, our life will be demanding, not easy. It will be challenging, not comfortable. It will be reckless, not safe.

One of the greatest challenges we face is to lay aside our need to control our life, especially our future. Are we open to the God of Surprises who seldom does things exactly as we expect? How sad it would be if we found ourselves saying, "My life has turned out exactly as I planned." How much better it is if we find ourselves saying, "My life took some drastic turns! I found myself doing things I never thought I could do, going places I never intended to go, befriending people I never thought I would. And who knows where God might lead me in the future!"

As difficult as vulnerability is, it is crucial for spiritual growth. The experience of our own vulnerability enables us to appreciate and respond to the vulnerability of others, especially the poor. M. Scott Peck writes in *The Different Drum*, "A life lacking the emotional upheavals of depression and despair, fear and anxiety, grief and sadness, anger and the agony of forgiving, confusion and doubt, criticism and rejection, will not only be useless to ourselves, it will be useless to others." The writer Madeleine L'Engle once said to a bishop, "My best writing has always emerged from my pain and sorrow." He replied, "Then I hope something terrible happens to you again soon!"

Kathleen Norris, in a recent interview, said this: "For some reason we human beings seem to learn best how to love when we're a bit broken, when our plans fall apart, when our myths of self-sufficiency and goodness and safety are shattered." Vulnerability can lead us to greater compassion especially for the poor. No wonder Henry Nouwen said, "The compassionate life is the life toward downward mobility." Vulnerability can also lead us toward greater community. When we experience our incompleteness, we realize how little we can do alone. We need both the challenge and support of one another to grow in love. And finally, vulnerability can lead us to greater trust in God. It is the midwife of deepened faith.

> ❦ *How have I experienced the God of Surprises in my life? How do I respond when my plans fall apart?*

Recently I read a poem entitled "In Praise of Boundaries." It inspired me to write this poem:

In Praise of Vulnerability

Glory be to God for vulnerability,
    for weakness and need,
    for limits and boundaries,
    for fatigue and fear,
    for they have the power to open my heart to the pain of others.

Glory be to God that I know I am not self-sufficient,
    that I experience (sometimes desperately) my need for God
    and for others who help me survive and grow.

Glory be to God for tears,
    for they remind me that people are irreplaceable,
    and that certain causes are worth dying for and living for.

Glory be to God for edges and parameters,
    for beginnings and endings,
    for shalls and shall nots,
    for they channel my energies into unselfish love.

Glory be to God when my plans fall apart,
    when I don't get my way,
    when the fault lines in my life become painfully visible,
    for then I will know in whom I place all my trust.

Glory be to God for our vulnerable Jesus,
    vulnerable Church, vulnerable community,
    and vulnerable little me.

CHAPTER 25

Against the Horizon of the Infinite

The month of November begins with the celebration of two great feasts, All Saints and All Souls. On All Saints Day we might ask ourselves, what exactly is a saint? One of my favorite definitions of a saint is this: someone who makes goodness attractive. On this feast, we can ask ourselves: Do we make goodness attractive? Do we make being a Christian attractive, appealing, inviting?

On All Souls Day and throughout the entire month of November we also remember in a special way all those who have preceded us into eternity. With every death, we are reminded that each day brings us closer to the end of our own earthly journey. That realization, rather than depressing us, hopefully gives us a greater appreciation of the value of each day and of the giftedness of each person.

In 2003, our religious community prepared for an upcoming provincial chapter. My thoughts at the time centered on these four words: come, dialogue, tension, and infinite. These are realities that enter into the lives of all Christians.

Come

The duties of the provincial chapter are sketched in article 150 in our constitutions. But perhaps the most powerful dynamic of a provincial chapter is just being together. Our being together will happen only if each of us makes a concerted effort, as far as we are able, to come to the pre-chapter meetings as well as the chapter itself.

I realize, there may be some reasons not to come. We could think, "I'm too old, I'm too young, I hate crowds." Come anyway! Or "I'm too tired, too discouraged, too busy." Come! Or "I have nothing to contribute. Nothing ever changes anyway." Come! The Good Spirit draws together. The Evil Spirit divides and fractures. The Good Spirit empowers us to do things together that we could never do as isolated individuals. Though none of us knows for sure what will happen at this chapter, we do know that something will happen. Part of it will never be captured in resolutions or summaries. It will only be experienced by our communal being together. Don't miss it! Come!

Dialogue

The Church recently lost a great man, Monsignor Phil Murnion. The sixty-five-year-old founder and director of the National Pastoral Life Center died of cancer in August. He is perhaps best remembered for his ground-breaking work with Cardinal Joseph Bernardin on the Catholic Common Ground Initiative. He was also known for his special love for anyone who was discriminated against—minorities, women, migrants, the homeless. In her tribute to him in the *Universe Bulletin* (September 12, 2003), Sister Kathleen Mary Ryan wrote that Monsignor Phil was "a pastor, a preacher, a promoter of human rights, a consummate communicator, and a 'priest's priest.'" She added, "I was lucky enough to call him friend."

Shortly before he died, Monsignor Phil sent a letter to all the bishops of the United States. He wrote it "as a dying person, with no time for the peripheral or accidental." In his letter, Monsignor Phil made this final plea to the bishops: "Dialogue, dialogue, dialogue!" He urged this while being well aware of its "cost and conditions." In fact, he noted that dialogue demands just as much asceticism as does "a spirituality of the desert or the cloister."

As we prepare for the chapter, I echo this plea: Dialogue, dialogue, dialogue! Truly listen to one another and speak openly and respectfully with one another. Keep the conversation going—no matter what. Let us dialogue while fully accepting the pain and frustration that often accompany such a task. For it is only through authentic dialogue that we will move closer to that "spirituality of communion" advocated so often by our Holy Father.

Tension

Tension is often viewed as something negative to be avoided or eradicated. But tension can be good, very good. (Even as I typed that sentence I cringed, knowing how hard it is for me at times to accept—let alone embrace—the tensions I experience in my life and ministry!) Recently I read the review of a book entitled *Contemplatives in Action: The Jesuit Way* by William Barry, SJ, and Robert Doherty, SJ (*America*, May 26 to June 2, 2003). In this book the authors examine seven types of tension that they believe are essential to "Jesuit living."

Their list prompted me to reflect on the tensions we sometimes experience as Sisters of Notre Dame and as Christians. A few I came up with are the tension between tradition and innovation, joy and sorrow, prayer and action, community and ministry, solitude and communion, poverty and the use of the world's goods for mission, the young and the not-so-young, trust in God and trust in one's talents, obedience and self-determination, chastity and affective friendships. The authors maintain that we do not want to snuff out either side of these tensions, nor do we want to maintain a static equilibrium between the two. Instead we want to live within the tensions in a way that is life giving and creative. While the ground between the two poles shifts, "the only way to survive whole and without neurosis is by trusting the hand of God to guide the seesaw." I wish for life giving tensions for all of us and for the ability to live within these tensions creatively. And I wish we may have the courage to stay on the seesaw!

The Horizon of the Infinite

As vital as a provincial chapter is, we must remember that it is only a chapter. The chapter is not the end-all-and-be-all of our life. It is not even the only way God can or will speak to us and direct us. We must resist the temptation to put unrealistic expectations on our coming together, our dialogue, and our ability to live within the tensions of our lives.

In a recent article, Father Ronald Rolheiser said something very wise: "We understand our lives best when we see them against the horizon of the infinite. Nowhere is this more important than in the belief that there is life beyond this one." He goes on to say that we do violence to ourselves and others if we expect this present life to give us all that we want and yearn for. If we stop believing in a future life, we put too much pressure on this life "to give us the full symphony." We then become frustrated with our lives and demand that our family, friends, sisters, and ministries give us something they cannot give—namely, complete fulfillment, full meaning, final satisfaction, heaven.

We must put this provincial chapter—and, indeed, our entire lives—against the horizon of the infinite. Although we can and should expect wonderful things from this chapter, we must not demand that it give us more than it can. Even after the chapter, we will still experience disappointments, bitterness, misunderstandings, gossip, and bad choices. But hopefully, because of our experience of chapter, we will be encouraged to bear these things with greater patience, understanding, and calm. As Father Rolheiser has said, "Outside a vision of faith in an afterlife, we cannot come to full peace in this life."

In her book *I Trust You God*, Sister Maria Alexandra Nolte shares a poem by Rabbi Jizchak that gave her strength as she journeyed from Germany to Brazil, to Italy and to South Korea, in her sixty years of ministry as a Sister of Notre Dame. The poem reminds us that our good God is the great constant amid the turbulence of our everyday lives.

Where I go—You!
Where I stand—You!
Only You, again You, always You!

When I am fine—You!
When I suffer—You!
Only You, again You, always You!
You, You, You!
Heaven—You! Earth—You!
Above—You! Beneath—You!
Wherever I turn—You!
On each end—You!

Only You, again You, always You!
You! You! You!

❧ *Can I see any good in the tensions I am now experiencing in my life? How do I keep before me the horizon of the infinite?*

CHAPTER 26

Prayer for Divine Intrusion

Christmas is a time to celebrate the coming of Jesus into our world and into our everyday lives. Here is a little poem I wrote for Christmas, but it can be used all year long.

Prayer for Divine Intrusion

God of love,
    come into my life.
Hold my hand, walk beside me, pat me on the back.
Help me up when I fall down,
    help me down when I'm puffed up.
Support me, encourage me, inspire me, disarm me.
Broaden my vision, expand my understanding, inflame my heart.
Listen to my cries, my sighs, my silence.
    Say "yes" to me. Say "no" to me.
Feed me, need me, hug me, bug me.
    Tickle me, awe me, mystify me.
Teach me to say, "I'm sorry." Teach me to say, "I forgive."
Set high standards for me. Make demands upon me.
    Never mistake my stubborn "No!" for my final answer.
    Free me from my tendency to wind around myself.
    Enlarge my world. Direct my attention to what really matters.
Fill my life with signs, and lead me to notice and interpret them.

Accept me as me,
  but keep prodding me to become a better version
    of who I already am.
Melt my coldness. Smooth my rough edges.
    Turn my thinking upside down.
Play with me, dance with me, weep with me, laugh with me.
Help me to live less cautiously.
  Reconnect me with my primitive folly.
Keep telling me to grow up. Keep telling me to be more childlike.
Give me a ton of patience,
  but never let me be completely satisfied with the way things are.
Deepen my trust in you. Increase my thirst for you.
Disturb me, perturb me, woo me, seduce me.
Love me, love me, love me. Amen.

❧ *What words or phrases from this poem speak to me today?*

CHAPTER 27

Messages about Love

When I think of Valentine's Day, I think of those little pastel, candy hearts that have brief messages on them like, "I love you…U R cool…Be mine." With this Valentine's Day letter, I am sending you something similar: brief messages of love. These messages are quotes about love that have personally touched my heart or stirred my imagination. May they do the same for you!

> Love doesn't make the world go 'round. Love is what makes the ride worthwhile. FRANKLIN JONES

> I feel there is nothing more truly artistic than to love people. VINCENT VAN GOGH

> Traveling in the company of those we love is home in motion. LEIGH HUNT

> What we avert our eyes from today can be borne tomorrow when we have learned a little more about love. DOROTHY DAY

> Truth without love is sterile. Love without truth is illusion. ANONYMOUS

> I am helpless before love. I could be bribed by a sardine. ST. TERESA OF AVILA

> Love is based on the belief in the reversibility of evil. THOMAS MERTON

Engrave this upon your heart: There isn't anyone you couldn't love once you've heard their story.   ANONYMOUS

When I stand before God at the end of my life, I would hope that I would not have a single bit of talent left and could say, "I used everything you gave me."   ERMA BOMBECK

Where there is love, there is disorder. Perfect order would make the world a graveyard.   ANTHONY DE MELLO, SJ

If there are poor on the moon, we will go there too.

MOTHER TERESA

Love is not an emotion. It is a policy.   HUGH BISHOP

❦ *Do any of these quotes resonate with my experience of love?*

CHAPTER 28

The Water of Life in Uganda

The Sisters of Notre Dame established an elementary school in Buseesa, Uganda, in 1995. A high school for girls was added in 2003. In March 2004, Sister Shauna Bankemper, the provincial of the Kentucky province, and I visited this school for about two weeks. Here are some of my impressions.

We landed in Entebbe and took a four-hour Jeep ride from the Entebbe airport to Buseesa. It was the roughest ride of my life. My first impression of Uganda can be summarized in one word: lush! Everything is so green! As we drove along, we saw many banana groves, lots of fascinating birds, a million goats, and one lone monkey.

Yesterday we were formally welcomed to St. Julie School by the students. The school has 169 students (P-3 to P-7) and fifty-six girls in high school. The entire student body met us at the gates of the school yard and, singing and dancing, led us into their all purpose room where each class welcomed us with song and dance. Several students played native instruments for us: drums and violin-like instruments that looked like a blend of a guitar, harp, and drum. We also toured the dormitories and the classrooms. It is amazing what the sisters have accomplished here in less than ten years.

Here are a few facts about Uganda.

- Fifty percent of the population is under the age of fourteen.
- Life expectancy is forty-eight years.
- The sisters have very little electricity here. Their stove runs on

kerosene and their tiny refrigerator on propane. They must transport their tanks all the way to Kampala to be refilled. They also have a little solar power that helps heat the water (a little) and runs the "light sticks" in each bedroom.

- Because Buseesa is located almost on the equator, it has twelve hours of daylight and twelve hours of night all year long.

- At night, the monkeys sound like huge bullfrogs

- Father Francis, the local pastor, was ordained two and a half years ago. In addition to the parish here, he has nineteen "out stations" he is responsible for. He uses a motor scooter to get to most of them since the roads are so terrible. He visits three of his "out stations" only once a year.

- The temperature during the day is in the high eighties. The people are praying for rain. The water tanks (which supply all the water for the school and convent) are almost empty.

It is Friday, March 12, and we continue to pray for rain. The sky is overcast, caused by dust, not moisture. We learned that the dust is really sand from the Sahara Desert. Huge windstorms are going on there, and the sand is being swept clear across the African continent. The sand settles everywhere. If you dust your room, sand covers everything a few hours later.

Two days ago, the postulants took Sister Shauna and me on a hike. We walked along a narrow path in the hot sun for more than two hours up and down the surrounding hills. Every now and then we came upon a mud hut. The postulants knew some of the neighbors, so they introduced them to us and translated for us. I was deeply moved by everything I saw: thatched roofs, naked babies, houses with no electricity, no windows, no furniture, and no water. Near each hut there were a few fields dug out of the brush. I saw tomatoes, potatoes, bananas, and pineapples and a few chickens. I couldn't help but wonder how these people manage to survive. As I went to bed that night, the images of everything I had seen came back to me. With my plastic bottle of clean water and my dependable flashlight, I felt like a millionaire.

There are three wonderful volunteers from Germany. The two young women, Miriam and (yes!) Melanie, teach and tutor in the school. The young man, Martin, runs the farm—no small task.

Miscellaneous notes:

- Eighty-nine percent of the population in Uganda lives in rural areas.
- Agriculture is the mainstay of the Ugandan economy.
- We have two watch dogs here. Caesar (mainly a Black Lab) watches over the convent and Police (mainly a German Shepherd) watches over the school. Both dogs are really needed here for security, especially at night.
- There are 16,000 miles of roads in Uganda. Only 1,200 miles are paved—and many of them are in terrible disrepair.
- Over forty languages are spoken in Uganda

We just returned from Mass at the local parish up the road. It was wonderful! The singing was lively, the harmony beautiful, and the drums powerful. It was not celebrated in English so I didn't understand a word, but I could tell when we were singing the "Lord have mercy" and the "Our Father." At the offertory, two women stood in front of the altar, facing the congregation. They each held a beautiful basket. One by one the people processed up the aisle and put their offerings into the baskets. Most put in a few coins, but I noticed one woman putting in a few onions from her garden. The Mass lasted about two hours.

We have been praying desperately for rain. This morning, at about 4:00, a storm came through with flashing lightning and roaring thunder. It poured for several hours. I could hear the rain running off the metal roof, into the gutters, and into the storage tanks. It was a blessed sound!

Here are a few more miscellaneous thoughts.

- The Sahara Desert is larger than the entire continental United States. All of the following combined are still smaller than the continent of Africa: the United States, Europe, China, India, and New Zealand.
- Since coming here I have seen no airplanes fly over. I haven't seen any motorized vehicles except for one truck. A few bikes and one

scooter have passed by. Almost everyone here walks or (for much longer trips) takes a taxi. The taxis are white vans with the words "licensed to carry 14" written on the side. But we have seen taxis with as many as twenty-five people crammed inside.

- Everywhere you look you see women and children carrying large yellow plastic containers on their heads. The containers are for water. They are a vivid reminder that virtually no one in this area of the country has running water in their homes.

On March 16, we had a three-hour tour of the farm. Martin, the twenty-six-year-old from Germany, is now in charge of the farm. It is a huge undertaking. The farm must produce all the food to feed 200 children three times a day, seven days a week, plus food for the sisters and lay help. The farm is located in two different places. Altogether it employs seventy workers, fifty percent of them are women. In fact, the foreman of the workers is a woman, which is unusual for this country. The workers must first clear the land of trees and brush, then plant the crops, tend them, and reap the harvest, all by hand. We saw more than one woman hoeing in the fields with a small child tied on her back. The farm is the largest single employer in this entire area, so it is good for the local economy.

What kinds of crops are produced here? I saw bananas, coffee, pineapples, beans, yams, Irish potatoes, cassava, ground nuts, maize (corn), oranges, passion fruit, pawpaws. There are well over 200 rabbits, a half-dozen goats, and nineteen pigs. Martin is building a new "piggery" which he hopes will soon be home to over 200 pigs. Martin explained the many challenges of farming in Buseesa. Monkeys steal the bananas, eagles and snakes eat the rabbits, lizards eat the bees in the hives, the land is so hilly that erosion is a problem, and disease is always a concern. Yesterday, for example, five healthy-looking rabbits were found dead in one of the hutches. This morning there were three more, so Martin is having one of the workers inoculate the rest of the rabbits before disease destroys them all.

Miscellaneous notes:

- Martin hopes by next year the farm will be one hundred percent organic.

- The male goat is named Attila. One of the females is named Cleopatra because she has dark lines around her eyes.
- Martin brought ten huge rabbits from Germany to breed with the other rabbits he has from New Zealand and California, so they can produce larger rabbits.
- In the field we saw a plant growing that is used for the treatment of Parkinson's disease. The pigs and rabbits know instinctively not to eat this plant. It is poisonous for them.
- We had rain again during the night. The water tanks are getting filled slowly but surely.
- The sisters have a satellite phone here that is much larger than a cell phone. They tell me a beam from the phone hits a satellite somewhere—and the signal ends up in Arizona, which transmits the call to its destination anywhere in the world. The sisters have to stand outside in their yard to use it.

Friday, March 19, is the feast of Saint Joseph. Bishop Deogratias paid a visit to our school on Wednesday. The bishop is a warm and friendly man who is extremely happy to have the Sisters of Notre Dame in his diocese of Hoima. He would love to have more sisters here to do pastoral work in the parishes, but learning the local language would be difficult (though not impossible).

We truly admire the work of our sisters here. They live without so many things most of us consider "necessities": radio, TV, washer/dryer, microwave, fans, air-conditioning, carpeting or tile on the floor, newspapers, nearby stores, paved roads, and an abundance of hot and cold water. Yet their spirit is upbeat and uncomplaining. They obviously love the people here—especially the children—and are using their gifts and talents to help educate this next generation.

Miscellaneous comments and observations
- Thirty-three percent of Ugandans are Catholic, fifty-two percent are of other Christian faiths, eleven percent are Muslim, and the rest are of other beliefs.

- Polygamy is common here. If a man has several wives, he sets up separate homes for each of them. If a Catholic is in a polygamous relationship, he or she may not receive the sacraments.
- The average woman in Uganda has six children.
- Bishop Deogratias has ninety-five priests in the Hoima diocese.
- The rainy season has officially begun and our water tanks are filled.
- The construction of the high school continues. It is behind schedule (obviously a problem that knows no national boundaries!). So far the latrines and dorms are completed, but the school itself has yet to be started. Meanwhile Sister Rita and Sister Anita Marie hold classes in two rooms at St. Julie School.

Sister Judith from Covington is here for a six-month sabbatical. She teaches high school science in the morning and then has free time. She has about twenty-six girls in her biology class and only four microscopes which she herself brought from the States.

We miss getting any world news. We did hear about the terrible bombings in Madrid, but otherwise, we have heard no other news since coming here. However, our prayer in chapel reaches beyond Buseesa every day.

The stars at night here are incredible! Every night Sister Shauna and I would venture outside with our "torches" (that's British for "flashlights"), stand in the middle of the courtyard, turn off our lights, and gaze for several minutes at the stars—so bright and plentiful. It will be one of our favorite memories of Uganda.

The postulants have given Sister Shauna and me our African names: Shauna was christened "Akiiki" which means "leader; royalty." I was christened "Amooti" which refers to a "flower arrangement." Tomorrow Sister Shauna and I will make the long four-hour bumpy trip to Kampala, the capital, and then south to the airport at Entebbe. We'll stay overnight at a retreat center in order to be at the airport in time for our eight-hour flight to London. This time we'll be flying during the day so we're eager to see Africa from the air, especially the vast forests and the great Sahara Desert.

The trip to Uganda, "The Pearl of Africa," has raised many questions in my mind. I wonder, "What happens to these children once they graduate from our school? What opportunities do they have to find employment or to continue their education?" I also ask myself, "How safe is Uganda?" There is rebel activity in the north and along some of the borders. I don't believe our sisters are in any immediate danger, but the political instability of the country is disconcerting. Another question: "Should we be making another foundation in Uganda soon—perhaps closer to a major city?"

In all, my time here has been a great blessing for me. I am inspired by what our sisters have accomplished here. I marvel at their dedication, self-sacrifice, joyfulness, and courage. My visit to Buseesa made me very proud to be a Sister of Notre Dame!

❧ *Does anything in this chapter surprise me or raise questions for me?*

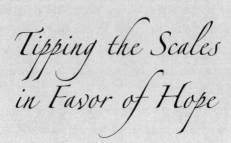

CHAPTER 29

Tipping the Scales in Favor of Hope

Recently a priest began his homily with these words from a Hallmark Easter card: "In a world of injustice, God, once and for all, tips the scales in favor of hope." The priest went on to say that God tipped the scales in favor of hope "through the resurrection of our crucified divine brother Jesus."

June is the month traditionally dedicated to the Sacred Heart of Jesus. As such, it seems an appropriate time to reflect on the virtue of hope. I offer you a few thoughts on hope, knowing that, if we believe the news media, the scales seem to be tipped in favor of despair, not hope.

What does it mean to hope? Hope can be defined in many ways. The dictionary says hope means "to desire something with the expectation of fulfillment." Hope, then, is not simply wishing. It is wishing coupled with the conviction that what we wish for will come true. As vital as hope is, however, it tends not to be showy. Macrina Wiederkehr, OSB, writes this about hope: "I was just thinking one morning during meditation how alike hope and baking powder are: quietly getting what is best in me to rise, awakening the hint of eternity within." Hope is so essential to our faith because it determines our basic attitude toward life and it fuels our endeavors to live the gospel. As Michael Downey says, "Hope is hospitality to challenge. Hope is a reach. It buoys up and carries into the future."

❦ *What is my definition and/or image of hope?*

Hoping is not easy. One Victorian-era funeral parlor used to advertise: "For composing the features, $1. For giving the features a look of quiet resignation, $2. For giving the features the appearance of Christian hope, $5." One reason hope is not easy is because it is not reasonable. As Norman Cousins says, "Hope is independent of the apparatus of logic." Let me illustrate this point with a story taken from the world of sports. (If you do not like sports, you can skip the next paragraph.)

Your baseball team is hosting a game. It is the bottom of the ninth inning and your team is losing 10 to 0—and there are two outs. Yet, by some magic, you have been given a glimpse of the future and you know with absolute certainty that your team is going to win the game 11 to 10. It is your turn to bat. As you step into the batter's box, how would you feel? What would you be thinking? Would you drag yourself to the plate and stand there with your head hung down in defeat? No! Because you know you're going to win, and that knowledge would affect even your posture! Would you be thinking, "Poor us! Poor me! I'm no good! I won't hit anything! We might as well cede victory to the other team and go home." No! You would step up to that plate with energy and confidence. You would be thinking, "Wow! This is exciting! I know I'm going to get on base! I know I am not going to strike out—no matter what! Maybe I'll get a hit! Maybe even a home run! Or maybe one of their players will make an error! Or maybe the pitcher will walk me—or hit me with a pitch. But I know I won't strike out! I will get on base! I will score!" The knowledge of certain victory would fuel you to play with enthusiasm. You would be excited and proud to be on a team that was going to achieve such a victory—against incredible odds! You would be eager to see how you and your team were going to achieve victory when things looked so totally bleak!

The story illustrates the power of hope. Our Christian faith assures us of the final victory of good over evil, life over death. It is hope that energizes us to play a significant role in bringing about that amazing victory. Hope helps us "play the game of life" with enthusiasm, commitment, pride, and a sense of wonder. The theologian Leonardo Boff wrote these words about hope: "Hope is the presentiment that the imagination is more real, and reality less real, than we thought. It is the sensation that the last word does not belong to the brutality of facts with their oppression and repression. It is the suspicion that reality is far more complex than realism would have us believe, that the frontiers of the possible are not determined by the limits of the present, and that miraculously and surprisingly, life is readying the creative event that will open the way to freedom and resurrection."

> ❧ *How does my hope influence my attitude toward life? Can I recall a time when hope filled me with energy and enthusiasm despite bleak circumstances?*

Hope is not something that just happens. It is something we deliberately choose to do. Hope is not synonymous with mere optimism either. It goes far beyond that trait which may or may not be part of our genetic makeup. After all, we are not responsible for our genetic makeup, but we are responsible for our basic attitude. We cannot excuse ourselves from hoping by saying, "I was born with pessimistic genes." No, we must ask God for hope. We must choose to hope. And once we choose, we must seek ways to nourish hope.

How can we nourish hope? One simple way is to hang around other hopeful people. Isn't this the underlying wisdom of Christian community: to rub shoulders with, pray with, walk beside others who believe, pray, love, suffer, weep, laugh, doubt, hope—just as we do? We also nourish hope by prayerful, daily pondering of the word of God. The psalms we pray every day, for example, are filled with hope. Keep praying them over and over again, even to the point of redundancy! One of my favorite expressions of hope from Scripture is one we pray regularly in the Divine Office (*Friday Morning Prayer*, Week II).

> Though the fig tree does not blossom,
>   and no fruit is on the vines;

though the produce of the olive fails
   and the fields yield no food;
though the flock is cut off from the fold
   and there is no herd in the stalls,
yet I will rejoice in the Lord;
   I will exult in the God of my salvation. (HAB 3:17–18)

Talk about a bleak situation! No figs, no grapes, no olives, no flocks, no herd! And yet the psalmist can still "exult in my saving God."

Now, that is hope!

❧ *What are some of my favorite expressions of hope from Scripture?*

An intrinsic link exists between hope and our daily celebration of Eucharist. Timothy Radcliffe, OP, former master general of the Dominicans, recently gave a lecture to the gathering of the National Federation of Priests Councils in Atlanta, Georgia. His talk was entitled "Priests and the Crisis of Hope within the Church." Father Radcliffe spoke of the need "to recover a genuinely Christian hope." He reminded his listeners that the church "was founded at just the moment it was breaking up." At the Last Supper, there was little reason to hope. Judas was about to sell Jesus, Peter was about to betray him, Jesus was about to be executed, and the rest of the disciples were about to run away. Years later, the gospels, too, were written during a second major crisis in the church, when the early Christians were being persecuted, imprisoned, and put to death. Says Father Radcliffe, "As Christians, we have no need to fear this present crisis of hope. Crises are our spécialité de la maison. The church was born in one." We nourish our hope by celebrating that first "Last Supper," that moment when everything was "breaking up." We make the Eucharist a priority in our life even if the time is inconvenient, the singing is lousy, or the presider is sexist. For it is precisely when we gather as a worshiping community and stand, sit, or kneel side by side with other believers—who are as flawed and as noble as we are—that hope continues to be born in us.

We nourish hope by catching glimpses of God's action in our daily lives. Isn't this what our daily examination of conscience is all about? It is not a time to record our faults or failings. Rather it is a time to "rummage" for God in the "stuff" of our daily lives. Not simply our personal lives but the lives of our families, congregation, nation, church, and human history itself. As some of you know, I love history. I believe, in one sense, we all should be historians. When I ministered with the Jesuit novices, one of the most important courses that the novices took was a Jesuit history course. I recall one Jesuit telling me, "Every Jesuit should take this course three times in his life: once as a novice, once when he celebrates his twenty-fifth jubilee, and again when he celebrates his fiftieth jubilee." His comment made sense to me. Nothing gives us a better perspective from which to view our current situation than a good sense of history. Nothing nourishes hope in God in the present more than to recall God's saving actions in the past.

❧ *What are some of the ways I nourish my hope?*

As I mentioned earlier, June is dedicated to the Sacred Heart, a devotion which focuses on God's unconditional love for us. Hope believes in the persistency of God's love. As someone has said, "God has made the eternal commitment never to switch off love." Hope demands that I make a similar commitment. Is my love persistent, all-inclusive, forgiving? Hope demands patience, or as someone has more accurately said, "Hope is revolutionary patience." When we hope, we believe in what is not yet seen. We believe, as Pope John Paul II has said, that "good is greater than all that is evil in the world" (*Crossing the Threshold of Hope*).

My prayer for all of us is this:

May we choose to hope despite the "brutality of facts"
    that bombard us every day.
May hope quietly enable what is best in us to rise.
May hope fuel our commitment never to switch off love.
May hope give us "revolutionary patience"

that will enable us to work untiringly
for a better, more just world.

And may hope help us trust more and more in a God whom we know—by personal and communal experience—to be good beyond all imagining.

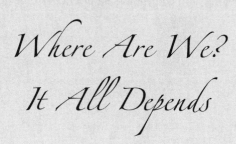

CHAPTER 30

Where Are We?
It All Depends

An important question to ask ourselves on a regular basis is this: Where are we? Where are we as Christians, and, more particularly, where are we as women religious?

The more I read about and study religious life, the more I am struck by a common thread that runs through much of the current literature—from the writings of the Holy Father to those of Sandra Schneiders, IHM, from Timothy Radcliffe, OP, to Marie Chin, RSM. This thread is expressed very succinctly in the document *Starting Afresh from Christ* (July 2002). It says this: Religious life is "the proclamation of an alternative way of living." Alternative to what? The document says alternative to "the world and the dominant culture." Let's reflect together on that for a moment.

Ronald Rolheiser, in his book *The Holy Longing*, says there is a madness in all human beings. He describes this madness as "an unquenchable fire, a restlessness, a longing, a disquiet, a loneliness, a gnawing nostalgia, a wildness that cannot be tamed, a congenital all-embracing ache that lies in the center of human experience and is the ultimate force that drives everything else." Marie Chin says that the greatest of these longings, which eclipses all others, is the longing for God. She goes on to say, "I have this growing conviction that the God Quest is indeed what my life as a woman religious is all about, and when the longing of my heart meets the longing of God, a holy conflagration happens."

As women religious, we have chosen to live this madness in a distinct and public way. When we are at our best, we do not deny this restlessness, this ache, this thirst. We embrace it. We do not try to fill our emptiness with stopgap measures such as food, medication, the buying of more and more "stuff," or sitting in front of the TV or computer for hours and hours. As women religious, we have made and continue to make what Marie Chin calls "elegant choices" for this madness within our souls. Those elegant choices flow from our vows: poverty, chastity, and obedience. These vows are the coordinates of the alternative way of living we have freely chosen by embracing religious life. Poverty is our resistance to the dominant values of greed and consumerism. Consecrated chastity is our alternative response to excessive individualism. Someone has said there are two kinds of people who walk into a room. The first says, "Well, here I am!" The second, "Ah, there you are!" Our chastity must be rooted in a healthy self-concept, yes—one that is healthy enough to reach out to others who so desperately need our love and our gifts. Obedience is an alternate way of using our freedom. Through obedience we channel our freedom into nurturing growth in others through our love and sacrifice, not through violence and coercion. The vows are a renunciation. But they are also a re-announcement of the gospel message that God loves us more than we can ever imagine. Experiencing that love impels us to love as Jesus did, even at great personal cost.

At the risk of being over simplistic, let me contrast the dominant values of our contemporary American culture with the values of our alternative way of living, which is rooted in the Beatitudes. By doing this I am not implying that all the values of our culture are evil. But the fact remains, many of the values of our age are in direct opposition to those of the gospel.

Dominant Culture

Use, buy, consume.
We live in a world of scarcity; there's not enough to go around;
    therefore we must hoard, stockpile, and build bigger and bigger barns.

Pain is bad; avoid it at all costs.

Since most pain comes from relationships,
    withdraw from others; seek ever greater privacy,
        independence, and autonomy.

God created the world billions of years ago;
    humans are meant to have dominion over all creation.

It's all about me.

Control others as much as possible,
    resorting to violence if necessary.

Gospel

Use wisely and gratefully, share, give away.

We live in a world of abundance;
    if we share the little we have with one another,
        we will have more than we need.

Pain, though difficult to bear, can be redemptive;
    it can call us to change; it can lead us to greater growth
        and compassion.

Yes, most of our pain does stem
        from interpersonal relationships,
    but so does most of our joy; keep interconnected with others
        at all costs; seek interdependence;
        Christianity is intrinsically communal.

God is still creating the world today;
    humans are invited to be co-creators with God.

It's all about us.

Love others; be the recipients of violence if necessary;
        return violence with love.

Because of our vowed commitment, we should be odd. We should look peculiar—not merely in our outward appearance, but, far more importantly, in the way we live and the choices we make as individuals and as a community. If we do not stand out against the culture in which we are immersed, then we must ask ourselves if we have gradually taken on the values of that dominant culture.

* *What do I do with the unquenchable fire, the disquiet, the restlessness, the wildness inside of me?*

* *Are there any signs that the God Quest is alive in me and in us? To what extent do I proclaim an alternate way of living? To what extent have we taken on the values of the dominant culture?*

It All Depends

So far, we have explored the question "Where are we?" Now I would like to explore the second part of the title: "It All Depends." "Where we are" is never static. It is in constant flux. Where we are is never in isolation. It is always in relation to God, others, our culture, and our environment. Where we are depends on many factors. I would like to make a few observations that touch upon three core topics: spirituality, relational living, and peace and justice.

By our vows, we have chosen to do a difficult thing: to live at odds with the world. Therefore, we must make the commitment to do the hard interior work necessary to live in such a way. What kind of interior work? Let me use a metaphor. This past year I had to do some physical therapy for my neck, shoulders, and lower back. Usually when I go for therapy in the second floor therapy room, other sisters are in the room getting therapy too. So there I sit in one of the cubicles getting ultrasound treatments on my neck and shoulders, while Sister A is in the next cubicle getting traction for her back, Sister B is in the therapy pool for her arthritis, Sister C is receiving treatments for her feet, and Sister D is in the corner doing exercises for her knees. One day I thought: What a graphic picture of who we are! We are all frail, we are all hurting, we are all in pain one way or another. Yet we have all committed ourselves to do the hard work of therapy to regain or retain our mobility and flexibility. We all set time aside to become healthier. I then had this thought: Are we just as committed to doing the hard work for our interior pain, our psychological hurts, our spiritual stiffness?

How do we do this difficult interior work? One way, of course, is our daily prayer which periodically includes an honest appraisal of where we are as individuals. Another way is daily Eucharist. As we open our hands to receive the Sacred Bread each day, we also open our hearts to the healing grace of Jesus. Other ways we do interior work is our monthly faith sharing, our annual retreat, spiritual direction, honest conversations with good friends, psychological counseling. The healthier each sister is, the healthier our local communities and our province will be. The more whole I am myself, the greater your chances are for being whole. The more spiritually alive you are, the better my chances are to be spiritually alive.

Having said that, I would like to add a caution: In community we must learn to live with a certain amount of hurts, disappointments, frustrations, misunderstandings, and personal slights. Every time I drive my mother to the grocery store in Chardon, we have to go over three speed bumps in the parking lot. They're terrible! They're so annoying! No matter how slowly I go, the bumps jolt us. Those speed bumps are a good image for daily community living. Community living is never completely smooth. These speed bumps, these "mini-upheavals" are always part of our daily living together. They are annoying, yes, and bothersome, but they are only speed bumps. They serve a purpose: to slow us down. So expect them, slow down for them, and then drive on. Don't let a speed bump stop the journey.

Fashioning a world based on gospel values is hard. Living a lifelong commitment of poverty, chastity, and obedience twenty-four hours a day, seven days a week is unbelievably challenging. If living religious life is not challenging, then maybe we aren't really living our vowed commitment as it is meant to be lived. Maybe we have settled for a neat, pinched, cozy little life instead of a wide and wild prophetic one. A prophet's life is rough. That's why prophets need other prophets so much. That's why we joined a religious community in the first place—

to be supported in our endeavor to live an alternate way of life that is humanly impossible. By living in community we are saying to each other, "I will be there for you!" We are also asking, "Will you be there for me?" There are countless ways of "being there" for one another: by living with each other and sharing the same space; by praying with and for each other; by showing interest in and concern for each other; by sharing a meal, going to a movie, engaging in a good conversation; by dialoguing with each other at meetings. In a talk she gave, Sandra Schneiders says if we attend community meetings, contribute to community dialogue, and embrace the statements and policies that grow out of our meetings, we are living a vital aspect of our vow of obedience.

The third core element is peace, justice, and our ministry and presence with the poor and marginalized. There is a direct link between the values of our dominant culture and the poor. Simply stated, the poor are the victims or the "collateral damage" of our contemporary way of living. Our obsessive consumerism, our pathological individualism, our preoccupation with power all contribute to building a world characterized by gross injustice, obscene poverty, and incessant war and violence. Perhaps I can express it best through a thought-provoking poem I came across recently called "The Only Sermon" by Andrea Ayvazian:

if we dug a huge grave miles wide, miles deep
and buried every rifle, pistol, knife, bullet, bomb, bayonet…

if every light-skinned man in a silk tie said
to every dark-skinned man in a turban
I vow not to kill your children
and heard the same vow in return

if every elected leader would stop lying
if every child was fed as well as racehorses bred to win derbies
if every person with a second home gave it to a person with no home
if every mother buried her parents not her sons and daughters

if every person who has enough said out loud I have enough
if every person violent in the name of God were to find God

we would grow silent, still for a moment, a lifetime
we would hear infants nursing at the breast
hummingbirds hovering in flight
we would touch a canyon wall and feel the earth vibrate
we would hear two lovers sigh across the ocean

we would watch old wounds grow new flesh
   and jagged scars disappear
as time was layered upon time we would slowly be ready
to begin.

Let us begin again. Let us pledge ourselves to continue to engage in the struggle to build an alternate world, one based not solely on the buying and selling of commodities, but on the Beatitudes. Let us work untiringly with and for the multitude of victims of our dominant culture: those who are poor, hungry, uneducated, unemployed, homeless. (Did you know that the average age of a homeless person in this country is nine years old?) We can't forget that our material affluence is built on the abject poverty of millions of our brothers and sisters all over the world. As the poem says, let us bury our guns and knives and bayonets. We all carry them, don't we? Sometimes they are words, looks, or gestures. Let us refuse to believe that genuine security can ever be based on military might. (Another horrific statistic: the United States has 6,000 active strategic nuclear warheads, 2,000 of which are on high alert!) Let us not believe the false god of war who says that we can make people good without loving them.

As the poem says, let us have the courage to say out loud, "I have enough. We have enough." Let us be still so we can hear hummingbirds hovering and we can caress an oak and contemplate the hallowed earth beneath our feet. (Did you know, one square foot of earth that is one inch deep holds on average 1,356 living organisms! Wow!) Begin again to have the kind of love Jesus showed when he reverently trod upon this earth, a love that is wide, deep, joyful, untiring. If we begin to do this, we will truly become bearers of compassion, peace and hope in our one world.

CHAPTER 31

The Virtue of Slowing Down

Theologian Doris Donnelly calls Advent "the most difficult season." She writes, "For all the high drama that surrounds Advent, the truth is we have a hard time getting involved in its mysteries." She suggests two main reasons for our difficulty. First, our society jumps the gun on Christmas and doesn't give Advent a fighting chance. Retailers who used to wait until after Thanksgiving to advertise their Christmas wares, now begin to bombard us with ads the day after Halloween or even earlier! It's hard for the haunting strains of "O Come, O Come, Emmanuel" to compete with the omnipresent pop versions of "Rudolph" and "Frosty the Snowman." A second reason why many of us find the Advent season difficult is that Advent is all about waiting, and waiting is a countercultural experience. Most Americans don't like to wait for anything, whether we're waiting for the computer to boot up, a frozen dinner to heat in the microwave, a red light to turn green, or our strength to return after surgery.

Recently I picked up a new book entitled *In Praise of Slowness* by Carl Honoré. While reading this book, I found myself saying to myself throughout a typical harried day, "Slow down, Melannie! Slow down!" This experience prompted me to choose this motto for my Advent season, a motto I suggest we might all share: Let's slow down! I say "let's" because, for better or for worse, we do have a tremendous influence upon one another. My hectic pace can cause you to rush more. Conversely, your calm and gentle manner can help me to live less frantically. I would like to reflect on slowness as a spiritual value, a value we might want to reclaim during this Advent season. First, I will share a few insights into slowness from Honoré's book. Then I will reflect on slowness and its relation to other values such as community, friendship, and prayer.

In Praise of Slowness

Carl Honoré calls himself a recovering "speedaholic." He first became acquainted with the "Slow Movement" through an incident with his little boy. Honoré was accustomed to reading a bedtime story to his son every night. As he did so, he found himself growing more and more impatient with his son's preference for "long stories read at a gentle, meandering pace." One day he spotted an article entitled "The One-Minute Bedtime Story." The article advertised books by various authors who had condensed classic fairy tales into "sixty-second sound bites." Honoré was about to order the books when he suddenly realized what he was doing to his life. He writes, "My whole life has turned into an exercise in hurry, in packing more and more into every hour. I am Scrooge with a stopwatch, obsessed with saving every last scrap of time, a minute here, a few seconds there. And I am not alone. Everyone around me...is caught in the same vortex."

Honoré suppressed his urge to buy the books of condensed bedtime stories. Instead, he continued to read stories to his son at a gentle pace. Then he began to reflect on "the cult of speed" in contemporary culture and gradually became acquainted with the Slow Movement. This movement, which originated in Italy as a protest against fast food, has become a world wide phenomenon. Advocates of the movement are not against speed per se. If speed is appropriate for a given activity, then that's fine, they say. But they strongly maintain that our love for speed has gone too far, becoming "an addiction, a kind of idolatry." And one tragic consequence of living a life of hurry is that we live superficially. When we rush, we fail to make real connections with the world and with one another. Says Honoré, "All things that bind us together and make life worth living—community, family, friendship—thrive on the one thing we never have enough of: time."

> ❧ *Is there any evidence that I am a speedaholic? (For example, how fast am I reading this reflection? What activities in my life deserve to be done more slowly? When was the last time I made a real connection with nature?*

Relationships take time and energy. I was reminded of this as I read Debbie Plummer's new book, Racing Across the Lines. In her book Plummer suggests that one way racial prejudice can be overcome is through forming friendships beyond our racial group. She tells of a TV sitcom where an African-American man encounters his new neighbor, a Korean. Both men initially dislike each other and openly display their prejudices. One day as they discuss their differences, they conclude that few people are willing to cross racial lines for friendship. One man sums it up with these words: "Maybe it doesn't have anything at all to do with prejudice; maybe we are just lazy."

Maybe we are just lazy. Relating to other people, as I have said many times before, is the hardest thing we do. In order to form relationships, we must go against our innate propensity for taking the path of least resistance. It is often easier, for example, to dismiss a relationship by saying, "We have nothing in common," rather than expend the energy needed to appreciate differences and to discover a deeper commonality. One of the main enemies of healthy relational living is hecticness. It is not making time just to be with one another. When we rush from one activity to another, gobble down our meals alone, drive our cars like maniacs, cut short our time for prayer, and barely have time to acknowledge one another's presence, then relationships suffer and community is jeopardized.

> ❧ *How much time do I set aside each week just to be with friends and with the persons I live with? Have I formed any friendships with individuals beyond my racial group, age group, faith group, or gender?*

I began this reflection by quoting Doris Donnelly who said that, for many of us, Advent is a "difficult season." The main reason Advent is difficult is because it calls us to change. Advent is a time not only to ponder Mary's pregnancy and her eventual bringing forth of Jesus into our world; it is also a time to challenge ourselves to become bearers of Jesus, to bring forth Jesus into our one world. Such a "pregnancy" and birth demand a change on our part. To bring forth Jesus, we must first be converted to new ways of thinking, new ways of being, new ways of acting that are more and more in line with the gospel. Our conversion, however, must not remain a private affair. As Donnelly writes, "The message of the incarnation is not an invitation to behold an innocent baby resplendent in inertia, but rather to take sides with a God who agitates for reform and shatters the status quo." During Advent, we are asked to venture across lines to befriend Jesus' "strange friends": those who are poor, weak, lowly, voiceless, dispossessed. We are asked to join forces with others who not only believe a better world is possible, but also labor to bring about that world, a world where love and forgiveness are "common currency" and where trust in God's promises prevails.

Mahatma Gandhi once said, "There is more to life than merely increasing its speed." May our slowing down this Advent be our gentle protest against the violence of our rushing world. May our slowing down give quiet, steady witness to the values of attentiveness, carefulness, patience, receptivity, and stillness. May our slowing down enable us to make real and meaningful connections with people, nature, work, art, and even God.

My prayer for all of us this Advent is this:

Come, Lord Jesus!
You who took time to notice lilies bobbing,
    birds soaring, and bread rising,
Come and slow me down.

You who took time to dine with acquaintances,
    go fishing with your apostles,
    and barbecue breakfast on the beach for your friends,
Come and slow me down.

You who took time to play with little children,
    listen to people's stories,
    and share their joys and sorrows,
Come and slow me down.

When my mind is stuffed with plans,
When my "To Do" list is pages long,
When I feel carried away by conflicting concerns,
Come and slow me down.

Give me the grace this Advent
    just to be,
    just to be with you,
    with people,
    and with my own hopes, fears, questions, and dreams.
Help me to bear you
    —slowly but surely—
    into the world,
    a world languishing and lovely,
    dark and delightful,
    sinful and saintly.
I ask these things of you through Mary,
the pondering Virgin,
your mother and mine.
Come, Lord Jesus, come!
Amen.

CHAPTER 32

Eucharist

Gathering, Listening, Loving

When Pope John Paul II declared the year of the Eucharist in 2004, he encouraged all of us to renew our appreciation of the Eucharist as the "source and summit" of our Christian life. In this reflection I would like to share a few thoughts with you on the Eucharist by focusing on these three aspects: gathering, listening, and loving.

The first thing we notice about our celebration of Eucharist is that we gather with others to celebrate it. In other words, Eucharist is essentially communal. For a long period in our Church's history this communal dimension of the Eucharist was not emphasized. In fact, for centuries there was a privatization of the Eucharist where individuals in the congregation silently recited their own devotional prayers, such as the rosary, while the priest "said the Mass" at the altar. Since Vatican II, however, there has been a renewed emphasis on the gathered community. In a Christmas message to his diocese, Bishop Blase Cupich of Rapid City, South Dakota, stated that the essence of the Eucharistic message is this: We are not alone and we are not on our own. Coming to the Eucharist, he said, "means stepping away from an approach to life that starts with the lie that we have to prove ourselves or save ourselves on our own." At each Eucharist we celebrate the fact that Jesus is with us—with the emphasis on us.

Coming together to worship is not always easy. In fact, it often entails sacrifice. The time of the liturgy may be inconvenient. We might have to travel, even in inclement weather, to where the liturgy is being celebrated. The church might be too cold, too warm, too crowded. If we worship with the same community for any period of time, we will soon become aware of the shortcomings of our fellow worshipers. This person sings off key. That person prays too fast. Latecomers and fussing children can be distractions. Even the presider can be a source of annoyance. He talks too loud. He talks too soft. He talks too long. Or we can be bothered simply because he is always a he. Deeper divisions within the gathered community may exist as well—differences among us in our understanding of God, Church, and liturgy itself. Yet faith tells us that it is precisely within this gathering—very human and maybe even very motley—that Jesus resides. In his book *Eucharist: Celebrating Its Rhythms in Our Lives*, Father Paul Bernier, SSS, goes so far as to say that "the most visible and powerful sign of Jesus' presence is the community that is gathered."

Our struggles to gather together for worship often mirror the ordinary struggles we face any time we try to work or live with others. Such struggles may tempt us to search for the ideal community or to abandon community altogether. At times like this it is good to remember that Jesus himself did not have the perfect community either. The "congregation" at the Last Supper included a traitor and a number of close friends who would deny or desert Jesus in his hour of greatest need. The truly amazing aspect of our gathering for the Eucharist is this: as imperfect as we all are, Jesus chooses to make his home in us.

❧ *Are there any signs that I privatize the Eucharistic liturgy? How accepting am I of the human communities in which I live, work, and worship?*

Listening

When we gather for Mass, we gather to listen to the word of God. The Church, in her wisdom, exposes us to a wide variety of Scripture readings throughout the year. Some Scripture readings are very consoling. I, for example, never cease to be moved by Psalm 23, the parable of the prodigal son, and Saint Paul's hymn to charity. But other Scripture passages are less appealing or even downright disturbing. Years ago when I took a Scripture course taught by Father Demetrius Dumm, OSB, at Duquesne University, he warned us against reading and praying only with those Scripture passages to which we are naturally drawn. Although it is wonderful to have favorite Scripture passages, we must be open to all of Scripture. In fact, the very passages that disturb us the most may be the ones we need to listen to the most.

At the Eucharist we also listen to the homily. Father Bernier writes, "The homily is not a learned exposition about what the Scriptures meant when they were written. Rather, it tries to face the community with what they mean to us now, wherever we happen to be." Some of us are blessed with hearing good homilies on a regular basis. Others of us may feel frustrated by what we hear or do not hear during the homily. Father Bernier suggests that when we reflect on the daily readings before or after Mass, we might try composing our own homily based on those readings. How would we preach these same readings? At the eucharistic liturgy we must also listen to the prayers and hymns we sing. Sometimes a word or phrase from these sources can have a great impact upon us.

- *Do I prayerfully reflect on the daily or Sunday readings? Which Scripture passages am I naturally attracted to? Which disturb me? Why?*

Loving

Another aspect of the Eucharist is reflected in a true story by Bishop Helder Camara of Recife, Brazil. One day thieves broke into a church in his diocese and pried open the tabernacle. They grabbed the gold vessels, dumped the hosts into the mud outside the church, and then trampled upon the hosts as they fled. The parish community was appalled by what had happened, and they asked the bishop to come and pray with them and say a few words about the sacrilege that had occurred. This is what the bishop said: "My dear people, we are gathered here to make reparation for a sacrilege that has been committed in our church. People broke into the tabernacle and trampled the body of Christ into the mud outside the church. This has saddened us, and rightly so. But, my dear people, in our country, Christ is daily trampled in the mud in the persons who make up his body, and no one sheds a tear."

Eucharist reminds us that Jesus is present not only in the hosts and in the gathered community; Jesus is present in all of humanity. As Father Bernier has said, "Jesus did not give us the Eucharist to feel good. He wanted it to enable us to be good...A properly celebrated Eucharist should bring about a cosmic change in our way of thinking and behaving." At Mass we not only listen to what Jesus taught, we receive strength to live as Jesus lived. The essence of Jesus' life was his selfless love, service, and care of others. Worship, then, is not simply a matter of doing certain practices—standing, singing, sitting, kneeling, bowing. Worship is a matter of living our lives in a Christlike and sacrificial way.

❧ *Are our choices as individuals and as communities consistent with what Jesus does in every liturgy—lay down his life for others? Am I as respectful of people as I am of the consecrated host? How is the Eucharist calling me to love and serve at this particular time in my life?*

The Sense of Belonging

In Father Bernier's book *Bread Broken and Shared*, he writes: "Can we celebrate Eucharist without being concerned about global poverty and injustice?" His answer, of course, is a no. During the past several years, we have all been moved by the devastation caused by natural disasters and terrorist acts. We have also been gratified by the outpouring of money and assistance to the victims of these tragedies. But the fact is that millions of the people affected by the destruction were already living desperate lives before the tsunamis, earthquakes, hurricanes, or terrorists ever hit. How mindful of them were we before the tragedy? How generous are we after their plight is no longer considered "newsworthy"?

❧ *Does our celebration of Eucharist reinforce our sense of belonging to the one, human family? Does it challenge us to see more clearly the direct relationship between our affluence and the destitution of so many other people?*

My prayer for each of us is this:

May we daily strive to grow in our appreciation
  of the amazing gift of the Eucharist.
May we willingly embrace the inconveniences,
  annoyances, and divisions that sometimes
  accompany our celebration of liturgy.
May our gathering together at the Eucharistic table
  nurture all the communities to which we belong.
May our attentive listening to the readings
  bring about a cosmic change in our way of thinking
    and behaving,
  especially toward our brothers and sisters in need.

CHAPTER 33

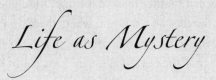

Life as Mystery

As we all know so well, the glorious feast of Easter celebrates Jesus' being raised from the dead, an event filled with incredible mystery. In this reflection I will share a few thoughts on mystery and the role it plays in our life of faith. We will also look at how our deep desire to control can sometimes get in the way of accepting the mystery of life. And lastly, we will explore some ways we can embrace the mystery of who God is.

Life as Mystery

The classic definition of religion is this: *mysterium tremendum et fascinans*, a mystery both disturbing and fascinating. Could we not say that life itself is both disturbing and fascinating? When things go as planned, for example, we are fascinated. When we spot a tiny, green shoot pushing up through a clump of dead brown leaves, we are fascinated. When we experience a chance encounter that leads to a lasting friendship, we are fascinated. When God feels close to us, we are fascinated. It is when life disturbs us that we sometimes get into trouble. When things don't go as planned, we are disturbed. When we see a loved one in pain, we are disturbed. When we behold a devastating natural disaster, we are disturbed. When God seems distant or absent, we are disturbed. Uncertainty and mystery can be so difficult for us that we sometimes we retreat into the certain, the known, and the familiar. As one family therapist put it, "Most people prefer the certainty of misery to the misery of uncertainty."

In her beautiful book *When the Heart Waits*, Sue Monk Kidd says that a certain amount of insecurity is not only inevitable in life, it is good for us. She writes, "Creativity flourishes not in certainty but in questions. Growth germinates not in tent dwelling but in upheaval. Yet the seduction is always security rather than venturing." Kidd goes on to say that total security eliminates all risk. "And where there's no risk, there is no becoming; and where there's no becoming, there's no real life. The real spiritual sojourners—the ones who touch the edges of life as well as the center–are people who risk, who let go."

When we let go and embrace mystery, we are admitting that we are not in control of life. God is. Scripture is filled with examples of individuals who surrendered control of their lives and who let God take over: Abraham and Sarah, Moses, Gideon, Esther, Jeremiah, David, and Joseph to name a few. The paragon of letting go, of course, is Mary. At the Annunciation Mary said to God, "Let it be done unto me according to your will." Says Kidd, "With these words, Mary let go of her own will and the security of her old life and yielded to the purposes of God." Mary's fiat epitomizes the essential movement of faith: the utter abandonment of ourselves to the mystery of God's will. Every time we surrender to the mystery of life–in both small and large ways–we are preparing ourselves for that ultimate surrender called dying. All our acts of letting go are but "dress rehearsals" for death, our final letting go.

The Culture of Control

We live in a culture that "idolizes" control. Have you ever noticed, for example, how many ads speak about control? They tell us: Use this shampoo and control your hair. Drive this car and control the road. Use this toothpaste and control the whiteness of your teeth. Invest with this firm and control your financial future. Take this pill and control your pain, cholesterol, digestion, weight, and sexual functioning. This worship of the "god of control" is expressed in other ways besides advertising. Practices such as abortion, euthanasia, and capital punishment are possible only in a culture that says we humans have the right to control life itself by deciding who is born and who is put to death.

Timothy Radcliffe, OP, the former superior general of the Dominicans, gave a talk at the World Congress on Consecrated Life held in Rome in November 2004. Radcliffe notes that never before in history has our world been under such tight control by so few nations. He maintains that the "national interests of a few countries call the shots." We live in the United States, the country that calls most of the shots. With our extraordinary economic and military power, our country attempts to control foreign governments and foreign natural resources, mostly to our own advantage. The terrorist attack on 9/11 has only intensified what Radcliffe calls "the culture of control." Since that attack, there has been an escalation in the gathering of information, more control of migration, and the decline of basic human rights.

What is the relationship between this culture of control and religious life? Radcliffe is strong when he says, "Religious life should explode into this culture of control as a burst of crazy freedom." We can see hints of what this means if we look at the life of Jesus. Though he, too, was caught up in a culture of control, he was amazingly free. His enemies tried to control him. His family members, thinking he was out of his mind, tried to control him. Even his apostles tried to control him. Jesus was watched, checked up on, and threatened, but he refused to submit to the culture of control. As Radcliffe says, Jesus "is our uncontrollable Lord." He submits only to the will of Abba, his loving Father.

> ❦ *Do I see any signs that I am serving the "god of control"? Do I see any signs that contemporary religious life is a "burst of crazy freedom" in our culture of control?*

Our Vows and Mystery

One way we religious embrace the mystery of life is through our vows. Our vows are a public commitment to remain open to the God of surprises, who sometimes interferes with our carefully laid plans and asks us to do things we never dreamed of doing. Through our vow of obedience we place our lives in the hands of God through the mediation of our particular religious congregation. In a very real way we hand over our lives to our sisters to do what we discern together. Sometimes the community, usually through those in leadership, will confirm what we ourselves have discerned to do with our gifts and talents. Other times the community will ask us to do something that seems to ignore or contradict what we ourselves have discerned. Obedience means we freely accept the fact that we are not the sole authors of our future. We have freely chosen to submit our personal preferences and even cherished dreams to the common good of the community.

The vow of chastity also encourages us to embrace God's mystery. By our vow we renounce any loving relationship that is exclusive. Instead we vow to give and receive love expansively, without the certitude of knowing who will be the givers and recipients of our love. I recall on more than one occasion being informed that I was being transferred from a place of ministry I knew and loved. I was deeply saddened that I would be leaving. I would miss the people I had grown to love. But I remember telling myself that there were going to be other people I hadn't met yet at my new place of ministry. I would grow to know and love them too and, hopefully, they would come to know and love me too. As someone once said, "God is always just a little in front of us on the road of life. God is looking back at us and saying, 'Come on!' God knows the way. Every day we are given the chance to say, 'Okay, I'm coming.'" Sometimes we say those words reluctantly, and God understands. But other times, trusting in our previous experiences of God's provident care, we say, 'I'm coming!' with great enthusiasm.

The vow of poverty calls us to live with a certain amount of insecurity, including financial insecurity. Paradoxically, in some parts of the world, one of the main attractions to religious life is precisely because it offers financial security. It is little wonder that the Synod on Religious Life has dared us to live a more radical poverty. Father Radcliffe says, "If people saw in our poverty a real precariousness, then what a sign of hope that would be!"

❧ In what ways has the vow of obedience or my "yes" to God led me to do things I never dreamed of doing? How expansive is my love? How different would our local faith communities look if we lived the spirit of poverty more precariously?

About twenty years ago, Father Ronald Rolheiser, OMI, made a retreat under the direction of an elderly sister. He admits that when he was young, he tended to make a cosmic tragedy out of every ordinary desolation and setback. Sensing his "Hamlet-type propensities," the sister gave him this little proverb: "Fear not, you are inadequate!" Rolheiser remarked, "It is healthy, humbling, and uplifting to accept the fact that we are not God and that we are not asked to be."

The writer John Shea says, "The Resurrection is the source of Christian joy and celebration, the music to which we ceaselessly dance, the song which we forever sing." As we celebrate the Easter mysteries, my prayer for all of us is this:

- that we become more comfortable with uncertainty, more at ease with ambiguity, more at home with mystery;

- that we connect more and more with Jesus' resurrection, the great source of Christian joy and celebration;

- that we dance more ceaselessly and sing more often; and

- that, in the words of James Finley, we accept life's ultimate "un-figure-out-able" nature that leaves us "delightfully perplexed, humbled, and grateful for a life we could not have planned if we tried."

CHAPTER 34

A Few Faces of Mary

As we turn our calendars to the month of May, we turn our thoughts to Mary. That question is impossible to answer. The theologian George Tavard knew how difficult it is to know Mary when he entitled his book *The Thousand Faces of Mary*. That title reminds us that every century and culture tends to interpret Mary in a different way.

One thing we know for sure about Mary was that she was Jewish. This means she believed in the God of Abraham and Sarah, a God who intrudes into human history, asks people to do difficult things, and keeps promises. She believed in the God of Moses, a God who hears the cries of the poor, frees people from their slavery, and enters into a covenant relationship with them. The gospels portray Jesus as a man with clear knowledge and a devout practice of the Jewish faith. It is reasonable to assume, then, that he was introduced to this faith by his parents. Mary followed the Torah, observed the Sabbath, recited prayers, and went to the synagogue. Even after the Ascension, Mary is shown as participating in the early Christian community in Jerusalem. But, as Sister Elizabeth Johnson, SCJ, says, Mary was never a Roman Catholic. She was a "Jewish Christian, the earliest kind of Christian there was."

❧ *What evidence is there in my life that I believe in the God of Abraham, Moses, and Mary?*

Mary was a village woman. She lived in a rural village where most of the people were peasants working the land or craftsmen serving their needs. The gospels tell us Mary was married to Joseph, the local carpenter. Some scholars put the Holy Family in the peasant class while others give them a blue-collar status. Either way, Mary's life was a difficult one. Like so many women, Mary struggled daily simply to feed and clothe her family. In addition, the political situation was a tense one, for her village was part of a country occupied by a foreign military power, Rome. Injustices, violence, and talk of revolution filled the atmosphere. We are indebted to our so-called Third World women theologians for calling our attention to the similarities between Mary's life and the lives of many poor women today. The flight into Egypt, for example, mirrors the flight of countless refugees in our own time. Mary's loss of Jesus because of an unjust execution parallels the experience of many women today who have had their children and other loved ones murdered by dictatorial governments.

Elizabeth Johnson writes, "It does Mary no honor to rip her out of her dangerous historical circumstances and transform her into an icon of a peaceful, middle-class life dressed in a royal blue robe." Mary lived during perilous times—just as we do.

❧ *How real is Mary to me?*

Mary was a woman of faith. Someone once said that Mary did not have the dogma of the Immaculate Conception framed and hanging on her kitchen wall. How true! Although Mary was a woman of profound faith, her faith was compatible with questioning. At the Annunciation, Mary asked two important questions: "What does it mean, Lord?" And "How can this be?" Joseph Cardinal Bernadin said that these two questions are our questions, too, as we face the myriad, complex movements of our lives. In her questioning, Mary is truly one of us. Like her we know times when we are troubled, confused, and even frightened by God's presence in our lives, which sometimes takes the form of God's apparent absence. "What does it mean, Lord?" is a question of doubt, helplessness, even despair. "How can this be?" can mean, "I don't understand…I can't do this…I'm not ready yet." Says Bernadin, "But, if nothing else, perhaps we will remember that even those moments are blessed by God's presence and Mary's example. For our very questions are a sign that God is a part of everything we do." Mary faced uncertainty and fear of the unknown future by trusting in God with whom she had a deep, personal relationship. During these times Mary had God. Only God.

❧ *Have I ever asked the same questions Mary asked?*

Mary is our companion. Elizabeth Johnson, CSJ, says there are two primary ways of relating to Mary: as intercessor and as companion. The intercessor model has dominated our tradition for many centuries. This model views God as a king sitting on a throne far removed from us. Because we are so small, insignificant, and far away from God, we need important people to intercede for us, to plead our case. Because Mary is the Mother of God, she is the most powerful intercessor of all. This intercessor model puts Mary somewhere between God and us.

But the companionship model places Mary alongside of us. Says Johnson, "In the companionship model, rather than the main action being prayers of petition from client to patron, the chief practice is attending to the memory of the dead that energizes hope." This does not mean that we do not pray to Mary or to the saints. "But this prayer occurs in the context of mutual sharing in the project of the reign of God." Real Marian devotion looks upon Mary as someone who helps us, yes, but not as someone who simply makes our troubles go away. Rather, Mary is someone who helps us live through our troubles as she did— with faith, courage and love. The new statue of Mary in our provincial house has Mary sitting down on a rock. It invites people to relate to Mary as companion. I have found it very natural in the evening, for example, to pull up a chair, sit beside Mary, and say, "How was your day, Mary?" And then I hear her ask me, "And how was yours, Melannie?"

❧ *Is Mary more intercessor or companion to me?*

Mary was prophetic. Another face of Mary is that of prophet. Nowhere is her prophetic voice heard more clearly than in her Magnificat. The Magnificat is the longest set of words placed on the lips of a woman in the entire New Testament. Mary begins her prayer by praising God her Savior who has done great things to her, poor woman though she is. As Kathy Coffey has noted, in her Magnificat, Mary "offers images of hope. She focuses not on the dastardly things humans have done but on what marvels God works." Mary proclaims that God has magnified not only her but all of the poor and lowly. Mary's image of God is not for the fainthearted. God shows might with his arm, disperses the arrogant, casts down the mighty from their thrones, lifts up the lowly, fills the hungry, and sends the rich away empty. In other words, for those who are comfortable with the way things are, beware! Coffey also notes that those of us who have grown up with the Magnificat forget how subversive it can be. It is so subversive that, during the 1980s, the Guatemalan regime forbade the singing of the Magnificat in public. Johnson writes, "This great prayer, a revolutionary song of salvation, places Mary in solidarity with the project of the coming of the reign of God whose intent is to heal, redeem, and liberate." In the Magnificat, Mary proclaims a new identity. Despite her lowly status she is a partner with God in bringing about God's reign.

How are we "in solidarity with the project of the coming of the reign of God" as Church, religious congregation, parish, family, and individual? How do we fall short?

Let us renew our love for and appreciation of Mary:

- as a religious woman who cherished and practiced her faith;
- as a village woman who nurtured hope amidst the dangers of her times;
- as a woman who wasn't afraid to ask questions because God was a part of everything she did;
- as our companion who walks beside us throughout the varied movements of our lives;
- as a prophet who invites us to partner with God in bringing about the reign of God on earth.

CHAPTER 35

Devotion to the Sacred Heart

What Does It Look Like Today?

Devotion to the Sacred Heart has been a venerable tradition in the church for several centuries. But what does this devotion mean to Catholics today? I do not know the answer to that question, but I suspect attitudes to this devotion are varied. Some of us find the devotion to the Sacred Heart to be very consoling and meaningful. Others may have difficulty with the devotion, stemming perhaps from some of the artistic representations of the Sacred Heart, the language of some of the prayers, or questions concerning the whole theology of reparation. But no matter how we view this devotion, we might ask ourselves this question: How does this centuries-old devotion to the Sacred Heart of Jesus resonate with some of the major movements in contemporary Christian spirituality? For me, three aspects of this devotion seem particularly relevant for our time. These aspects can be summarized by three adjectives: the Sacred Heart of Jesus is human, wounded, and loving.

A Human Heart

Historically, devotion to the Sacred Heart began somewhere between the eleventh and thirteenth centuries when Christian spirituality began to focus more and more on the humanity of Jesus. The first thing we notice about the Sacred Heart of Jesus, therefore, is that Jesus' heart is a human heart, like mine, like yours. This emphasis on the humanity of Jesus is not foreign to us, since Vatican II has given impetus to an increasing emphasis on Jesus' humanity. The Pastoral Constitution on the *Church in the Modern World*, for example, states very clearly that Jesus loved with a human heart.

Devotion to the Sacred Heart underscores the humanity of Jesus. (A while ago I saw a typo in a religious book. Instead of the Sacred Heart of Jesus, the book said the Scared Heart of Jesus! I had to smile at that mistake. But after thinking about it for a little while, I thought the mistake was not such a bad one, for I am sure there were times when Jesus' human heart was scared!) In his book *The Holy Longing*, Father Ronald Rolheiser devotes a whole section to the significance of Jesus' humanity. He writes, "The central mystery within all of Christianity, undergirding everything else, is the mystery of the Incarnation." He goes on to say that the Incarnation was "no one-shot incursion by God into human history….The Incarnation is still going on, and it is just as real and as radically physical as when Jesus of Nazareth, in the flesh, walked the dirt roads of Palestine." The writer Alice Camille says something similar. "Once divinity took up residence in the flesh, it was an address God never abandoned."

This means that the Incarnation did not end with Jesus' ascension into heaven. As Rolheiser says, "God is still here, in the flesh and continues to dwell among us. In the body of believers and in the Eucharist, God still has physical skin and can still be physically seen, touched, smelled, heard, and tasted." As we know so well, the phrase Body of Christ extends beyond Jesus' historical body to include the Eucharist and the whole of humanity. This way of viewing the Incarnation has important implications for our lives. It impacts our prayer, discernment, ministry, daily living, and so on. We make Saint Teresa's words our own: "Christ has no body now but yours…no hands…no feet…no eyes…but yours."

> ❧ *How does my belief in the incarnation impact my prayer, discernment, ministry, and daily living?*

A Wounded Heart

Author Wendy Wright notes that, in medieval times, when people became more familiar with Jesus as a human person, "They wondered what he thought about things. They began to wonder what he experienced, especially when he hung there on the cross….And they imagined the wounds…the pierced side. Especially the side." Another aspect of the Sacred Heart, therefore, is that it is a wounded heart. Just like mine. Just like yours.

Father Richard Rohr has said that Jesus "is the teacher of vulnerability more than anything else." Jesus' heart was most vulnerable and most wounded as he hung on the cross and experienced doubt, betrayal, and even apparent abandonment by God. His cry, "My God, my God, why have you forsaken me!" encapsulates his despair. Ronald Heifetz, on the faculty at Harvard University, makes an interesting observation about Jesus' anguish on the cross. He says that nearly in the same instant that Jesus expresses his sense of abandonment, he expresses profound compassion as he utters, "Father, forgive them for they know not what they do." Heifetz notes that, despite his personal anguish, "Jesus remained open." Heifetz concludes, "A sacred heart means…the capacity to encompass the entire range of human experience without hardening or closing yourself. It means that even in the midst of disappointment and defeat, you remain connected to people and to the sources of your most profound purposes."

As provincial for six years, I was often with sisters when they were in great pain whether physically, psychologically, or spiritually. Sometimes a sister would say to me, either then or later, she sensed that God was very present amid her anguish. When we are most vulnerable, God has easier access to our heart and soul. As Father Phil Murnion once said, "It is in concrete, imperfect, even sinful activities that we are most likely to catch a glimpse of the grace of God." Devotion to the Sacred Heart reminds us that our woundedness can be a conduit of God's grace. The "fractures" in our own lives can be the openings through which God's grace can pour in. These same "fractures" can also be the openings from which our own love pours forth onto others. Many years ago I realized that the individuals I admired the most all had one thing in common: They had all suffered—sometimes terribly. Yet somehow their personal anguish did not harden them or close them off from life. Rather they had allowed their pain to transform them into people of unbelievable warmth, understanding, and love.

❧ *Have I ever experienced the presence of God during a time of anguish or pain? Has my vulnerability helped me to be more compassionate and understanding?*

A Loving Heart

The American psychiatrist Harry Stack Sullivan defines healthy, adult maturity as "a state in which tenderness prevails." I like that. It reminds me that devotion to the Sacred Heart is, in essence, all about tenderness, all about love. For centuries the great symbol of love has been the human heart. Devotion to the Sacred Heart proclaims God's unconditional love for us. It also challenges us to love as Jesus did. This means our love must be expansive, continually stretching beyond where it is today. In his Apostolic Letter, *Novo Millennio Ineunte*, Pope John Paul II speaks about the importance of the "spirituality of communion." This is the ability to view everyone on earth as our brothers and sisters, as "those who are part of me" (n. 43). If we love as Jesus did, our love must be all inclusive, too. On the cross, Jesus' love encompassed even his murderers.

Though our love must be expansive, it must also be close to home. As the old adage says, "Charity begins at home." In her fascinating book, *Jesus CEO*, Laurie Beth Jones describes what she calls "The Sprinkler Phenomenon of Management." She says that if you look at a sprinkler head in a lawn, you sometimes see that the grass immediately around the head is brown. Ironically, the grass closest to the source of the water often gets no water, whereas the grass farther away receives plenty of water and flourishes. Jones maintains that some managers can overlook or ignore the people closest to them. Maybe the sprinkler phenomenon applies not only to managers but also to all of us who call ourselves lovers. In our loving, do we sometimes overlook the people closest to us? Do we pour out our love on others—the people we serve in our ministry, for example, or the strangers we encounter at the mall—while overlooking the very persons we live with or the individuals who minister alongside us?

❦ *How expansive is my love? Is anyone excluded? Does the sprinkler phenomenon of loving apply in any way to my loving?*

A little kindergarten girl once said, "Jesus is God's show-and-tell." What a profound statement that is. Devotion to the Sacred Heart of Jesus can be one concrete way of reminding ourselves that our own hearts, like the heart of Jesus, are human, wounded, and loving.

Let us pray:
Heart of Jesus, you are human.
Give me a greater appreciation of your incarnation
    extended into my time and place.
Help me find God
    in all of humanity.

Heart of Jesus, you are wounded.
Give me the courage to face my own sinfulness.
May the fractures in my life
    be openings through which your grace can pour.
And may my personal pain
    never harden my heart or close me off from others.
Rather, may my hurts and anguish
    transform me more and more
    into a person of warmth and understanding.

Heart of Jesus, you are loving.
Help me love ever more expansively and inclusively.
At the same time, help me discover creative ways
    to lavish my love on those who are closest to me.
"Within your Heart, O Jesus, my heart alone can rest."

Index

The number indicates the number of the chapter.

Advent, 15, 20, 31
adversity, 14, 16
All Saints, 25
ambiguity, 7, 8
Annunciation, 4, 17, 20, 33
art, 10
attitude, 12

Beatitudes, 30
beauty, 10, 13, 18
Bernadin, Joseph Cardinal, 34
borders, 19, 20
Buddhist seminary, 19

celibacy (consecrated chastity), 3,
    21, 30, 33
chapter, 25
charism, 13
Chesterton, G.K., 16, 17
Christmas, 20, 26
Church, 29, 32
commitment, 13, 30, 33
common good, 13, 20
community, 1, 7, 10, 18, 20, 21, 30,
    32
compassion, 20, 21, 24
consumerism, 10
control, 18, 24, 33
creation, 13, 18, 21, 22, 23

dialogue, 25
diminishment, 24
DMZ, 20

earth, 13, 18, 23
Easter, 5, 11, 23, 33
Eucharist, 29, 32
ecology, 13, 18, 23

fear, 5, 15
forgiveness, 18, 35
friendship, 21
freedom, 11

Gandhi, Mahatma, 31
God's call, 8
grace, 18
gratitude (see thanksgiving)

Hellwig, Monica, 20
Henschel, Abraham, 3
Holy Spirit, 7, 18, 24
homelessness, 21
hope, 1, 29
Hopkins, Gerard Manley, 18
Houselander, Caryll, 4
human condition, 1, 25, 35
humor, 17
hunger for the more, 3

Incarnation, 20, 31, 35
India, 2
individualism, 10, 13, 30

John Paul II, 13, 14, 29, 32, 35
joy, 17
justice, 2, 5, 14, 30, 32

Korea, 19, 20

laughter, 17
leisure, 23, 31
Lent, 3, 10, 16, 21, 32
Lindbergh, Anne Morrow, 9, 24
listening, 32
longing, 3, 30
love, 9, 20, 24, 27, 32, 35

Mary, 4, 17, 20, 33, 34
Mass (see Eucharist)
Merton, Thomas, 3, 5, 9, 23
metaphor, 12
militarism, 10
ministry, 30
mystery, 33

nature, 22, 23
Newman, John Henry, 23
9/11, 14, 18
Nouwen, Henri, 3

obedience, 3, 30, 33

pain, 1, 14, 16, 24
Pentecost, 7, 24
poverty, 2, 3, 24, 28, 30, 32, 33
peace, 5, 21, 30
poetry, 2, 3, 16, 18, 20, 22, 24, 25, 26, 30, 31, 35

racism, 10, 31
Rahner, Karl, SJ, 8, 15
restlessness, 3, 30
resurrection (see Easter)

Sacred Heart, 9, 35
St. Augustine, 3, 5
St. Joseph, 15
St. Julie Billiart, 8, 17
sacrifice, 18
service (see also love and ministry), 1, 4, 8
sexism, 10
slowing down, 10, 31
South Korea, 19, 20
suffering (see also pain), 14, 16, 24, 34, 35

Tagore, 3
tension, 25
terrorism, 14, 16
thanksgiving, 6, 14
time, 6
transformation, 16
truth, 1

Uganda, 28

Valentine's Day, 9, 22, 27
vows, 3, 13, 21, 30, 33
vulnerability, 24, 35